D1338623

The Black Woman in American Society
A Selected Annotated Bibliography

Lenwood G. Davis

G. K. HALL & CO., 70 LINCOLN STREET, BOSTON, MASS.

Copyright © 1975 by Lenwood G. Davis

Library of Congress Cataloging in Publication Data

Davis, Lenwood G
   The Black woman in American society.

   Includes index.
   1. Afro-American women—Bibliography.
I. Title.
Z1361.N39D36 [E185.86]   016.973'04   75-33275
ISBN 0-8161-7858-5

This publication is printed on permanent/durable acid-free paper.
MANUFACTURED IN THE UNITED STATES OF AMERICA

TO TATIA

A FUTURE

BLACK WOMAN

Foreword

For more than one hundred years, the Black woman has been a positive force in the development of American Society. As a subject of research she has been neglected by both white and black scholars. Today, however studies are appearing in print relating to Black women. Some institutions of higher learning are now offering courses on the Black woman. Research centers on women's history include factual data on Black and Third World women in their extensive collections, documenting the contemporary history of women, as well as that of the past. The Women's History Research Center, Inc. in Berkeley, California; the Afro-American Women's Collection at Bennett College, Greensboro, North Carolina and the Arthur and Elizabeth Schlesinger Library on the History of Women in America are examples or organized research collections on women. Since 1968, The Black Women's Community Development Foundation based in Washington, D.C. has kept abreast of what the present day Black woman is doing to initiate and sustain various community projects and through its Fellowship Program has aided Black women to develop into outstanding scholars.

Special issues of periodicals such as Ebony, Black World, Black Scholar, Essence, Encore, The Massachusetts Review, Black Enterprise, Women's Education and others have served to draw attention to the achievements and problems of Black women, past and present. Two of these periodicals, Essence and Encore are edited by Black women.

Alexander Crummell published in 1883-"The Black Woman of the South, Her Neglects and Her Needs." Ten years later in 1893, Lawson Andrew Scruggs' Women of Distinction and Monroe Alphonse Majors' Noted Negro Women, Their Triumphs and Activities described the achievements of many Black women in various fields of endeavor. In the same year that Francis Ellen Watkins published Iola Leroy, or The Shadows Uplifted, probably the first full-length novel by a Black woman, Anna Julia Cooper made a strong plea for her race and sex in-Voice of the South, by a Black Woman of the South. Both appeared in 1892. The Black Woman in America, by Robert Staples; Tony Cade's The Black Woman; An Anthology; Eleanor Flexner's Century of Struggle; Black Women in White America by Gerda Lerner; Keeping the Faith: Writings by Contemporary Black American Women edited by Pat Crutchfield Exum along with countless articles by and about Black

FOREWORD

women are at last revealing their accomplishments, problems and place
on the ladder of history.

The literature on Black women is appearing rapidly and it is not
easy to keep up-to-date on what has appeared and where. Lenwood G.
Davis has provided this basic reference tool in which he has brought
into one place a considerable number of printed works on diverse aspects of the life and history of Black women. He has also included
other data of prime interest. It is to be hoped that he will supplement this bibliography at a later date and include citations not
identified or selected for this present volume and include new references currently appearing. Certainly, Professor Davis' Bibliography
on Black women will be useful to many individuals, organizations and
libraries, especially during this Women's International Year.

DOROTHY B. PORTER

Contents

Introduction

Over the past few years there has been a tremendous amount of
attention given to the study of women in American Society. Yet
Black women, as usual, were not included in those studies. The traditional reasons given for omitting Black women were that they should
be studied along with Black men, and that there was not enough available materials on them. Since books, articles, magazines, and other
literature on Black women are appearing regularly, few people can now
say that there is not enough available materials on them. Even Black
women's causes and conferences are held almost monthly. Moreover, a
number of colleges and universities are presently offering courses on
or related to Black women. Institutions of higher learnings, and
American society are finally admitting that Black women are a legit-
imate subject of inquiry.

This bibliography, like any bibliography, has as its main short-
coming the omission of certain works. I am sure some will want to
know why I did not include certain materials. There are two reasons. First, I included only those works that I personally read, or
that were read by the persons who assisted with the annotations.
Second, I was unaware of the existence of certain works. In spite
of the shortcomings of this work, I still feel that this annotated
bibliography is one of the most comprehensive and exhaustive ever
compiled.

It is primarily designed as a reference tool for those who wish
to learn more about the life and achievements of the Black woman in
the United States. The materials listed cover every period of the
Black woman's existence in America from the earliest time to the
present.

I have included many autobiographies and autobiographical works
because they are an invaluable source of Black life and conditions.
In these works, one may get an inside view of how Blacks felt about
the larger society. They include achievements as well as disappointments, pains, sufferings, human miseries and racism of America.
Here we get a better understanding of Black women's most inner feelings and thoughts. It is regrettable that more Black women did not
write about themselves. Most people are aware that autobiographies
are more subjective than objective. They are useful in helping us

ix

Introduction

know more about Black women and Black people because they are pri-
mary sources and much can be learned from those works. These works
take on greater significance when one realizes that few people,
white or Black, have written about their life and times. It is the
hope of this author that this study will inspire many more Black
women to write their life story.

The works cited, pertain to the broader aspects of the Black
woman whether she is seen as a Black, woman, slave, mother, lover,
wife, worker, leader, or head of a family. The citations include--
autobiographies, sketches, articles, significant sections or chapters in books, all of which are in some way related to the Black
woman in the United States, past and present.

Many of the books and articles cited are out of print. However,
the serious researcher can find them in various libraries--colleges
and universities, as well as public. Some of the out of print books
have been and are being reprinted. Hence, many more of the books
should be readily available.

One writer has pointed out "Black women have been doubly victim-
ized by scholarly neglect and racist assumption. Therefore, it is
the task of historians, both Black and white, to give Black women
their proper role in history." During slavery they were exploited,
both sexually and physically by white men. Yet, Black women still
survived this degradation so much, that her strength and racial
pride has been a stabilizing force in the Black family and Black
community all through the years.

The noted Black scholar, W. E. B. Dubois best summarized Black
women's heritage in America when he stated: "No other women on
earth could have emerged from the hell of force and temptation which
once engulfed and still surrounds Black women in America with half
the modesty and womanliness that they retain."

Because of the present interest in Black life and history in
general, and the Black woman in particular, it is timely for an annotated bibliography of this kind to be compiled. Perhaps, the most
comprehensive to date is Johnnetta Cole's, "Black Women in America:
An Annotated Bibliography," The Black Scholar, December 1971. Another excellent work, The Black Family and the Black Woman: A Bibliography, was published by the Library Staff and the Afro-American
Studies Department of Indiana University, (1972). A recent work on
Black women is Ora Williams' American Black Women in the Arts and
Social Sciences: A Bibliographic Survey, (1973). There is an ex-
cellent bibliography in Gerda Lerner's Black Women in White America:
A Documentary History, (1972). There are working bibliographies in
a number of books on the Black woman: Joyce A. Ladner's Tomorrow's
Tomorrow: The Black Woman, (1971), and Sylvia Dannett's Profile of
Negro Womanhood, (1964-1966). One of the most recent books on the
Black woman is Robert Staples' The Black Woman in America: Sex,

Introduction

Marriage and the Family, (1970). It contains an excellent bibliography. The Woman's Bureau of the United States Department of Labor publishes occasionally Bulletins on the Black woman. Most of these Bulletins are included in this work.

Obviously, any work of this endeavor requires the assistance of many people and many hours. It is impossible to name all persons that assisted in this work, however, I must express special acknowledgement to the following persons who assisted with the annotations: Ms. Evelyn Crowell of Portland State University's Library; Dr. Lee P. Brown and Greg Benton of Howard University; Dr. Russell Bringnano of Carnegie-Mellon University; and Gary Baker of the Ohio State University. The secretaries, Sylvia Noel, Penny Martin, Judie Strain, Yolanda Robinson, and Patt Myles of the Department of Black Studies at The Ohio State University. I am indebted to the entire staffs of the Ohio State University Library, Howard University, Multnomah County Library, Portland State University Library, and Livingstone College Library. I especially wish to thank Dorothy B. Porter for not only writing the Preface, but also for her editorial assistance.

I take full responsibility, however, for all errors. I also welcome any corrections or additions.

ANNOTATED BOOKS

1 Abdul, Raoul. <u>Famous Black Entertainers of Today</u>. New York:
   Dodd, Mead & Co., 1974.
      Several Black women are included: Martina Arroyo, inter-
   national opera star; Gloria Foster, actress; Aretha
   Franklin, Queen of Soul; Micki Grant, composer-lyricist and
   performer; Diana Ross, singer-actress; and Cicely Tyson,
   actress. The author had personal interviews with all of the
   women mentioned. Also includes a photo of each person.

2 Adams, Effie Kay. <u>Experiences of a Fulbright Teacher</u>.
   Boston: Christopher Publishing House, 1956.
      The story of a Black American woman's teaching experience
   as a Fulbright Scholar in Pakistan. Gives a day by day
   account of her experience. The trip took place September
   14, 1952 and ended May 28, 1953.

3 Adams, Elizabeth Laura. <u>Dark Symphony</u>. New York: Sheed and
   Ward, Inc., 1942.
      An autobiography of a Black woman's quest for Christ.
   Tells of her many disappointments with Catholicism before
   she finally became a Catholic. She sees life as a "Dark
   Symphony" with all her imperfections, zeal and few virtues.

4 Adoff, Arnold, Editor. <u>My Black Me: A Beginning Book of</u>
   <u>Black Poetry</u>. New York: E. P. Dutton & Co., Inc., 1974.
      Compilation of poems reflecting thoughts on being Black.
   Many are by Black women: Lucille Clifton, Jackie Earley,
   Julia Fields, Carol Freeman, Nikki Giovanni, Kali Grosvenor,
   Vaness Howard, Mae Jackson, Barbara Mahone, Carolyn Rogers,
   and Sonia Sanchez. There are also short biographical
   sketches of each poet as well as a list of her other works.

5 Albert, Octavia Victoria Rogers. <u>The House of Bondage: Or,</u>
   <u>Charlotte Brooks and Other Slaves</u>. New York: Hunt and
   Eaton, 1890.
      A panoramic exhibition of slave-life, emancipation and the
   results of each told by ex-slaves in their own words. Mrs.
   Albert was born a slave in Georgia in 1853, and was later

1

(Albert, Octavia Victoria Rogers)
educated at Atlanta University. Shows the unrelenting
patience of Blacks and their faith in God. One of the few
early books in which former slaves tell about their experiences under the system of slavery from a slave's point of
view.

6   Albertson, Chris. Bessie. New York: Stein and Day, 1927.
A biography of Bessie Smith, called by many the "Greatest
Blues Singer in the World." Unlike some biographies of
Miss Smith, the author used a number of Black newspapers
and periodicals from 1915 to 1937. Also tells of the times
and conditions affecting Black Americans between 1900-1937.
A number of photos of Miss Smith are included in the book.

7   Alexander, William T. History of the Colored Race in America.
Kansas City: Palmetto Publishing Co., 1887.
There are brief references to Black women throughout the
book as well as a chapter on "Woman's Higher Education."

8   Alpha Kappa Alpha Sorority. Heritage Series. Chicago: Alpha
Kappa Alpha, 1971. Grati.
Contemporary biographical sketches of outstanding Black
women who are members of this Black Sorority. This was the
first sorority to be established by Black college women in
the United States.

9   Anderson, Marion. My Lord What a Morning, An Autobiography.
New York: Viking Press, 1969.
A deeply moving and inspiring account of Anderson's life
from childhood in Philadelphia to her rise as a singer of
international acclaim. Her philosophy of race relations
and the many obstacles that she had to overcome to be
accepted as a Black and as a woman are discussed. Tells of
her hope in the future of her people and her country.

10   Anderson, Rosa Claudette. River, Face Homeward: An Afro-
American in Ghana. New York: Exposition Press, 1966.
An autobiographical sketch of a Black American's travels
in Africa and her friendship with several Africans. Mrs.
Anderson summarizes her trip, "The Afro-American must know
his beginnings, like all other peoples; and in knowing he
will no longer bow his head in shame, but hold it up high
in honor among his fellow man."

11   Angelou, Maya. I Know Why the Caged Bird Sings. New York:
Random House, 1970.
A beautiful, readable and intimate personal narrative.
Often comical, often tragical, her recollections of people
and events add greatly to the literature of Black people
in America.

12   _____. Gather Together in My Name. New York: Random House,
      1974.
          A continuation of Miss Angelou's earlier autobiography, I
      Know Why the Caged Bird Sings. Covers the years after 1945
      when she was employed in a variety of jobs--cook, waitress,
      and dancer--while supporting herself and her child. Al-
      though this work is not as forceful as her earlier book, it
      still gives the reader a better understanding of a complex
      Black woman.

13   Aptheker, Bettina. The Morning Breaks: The Trial of Angela
      Davis. New York: International Publishers, 1975.
          One of the latest books about the life and time, and trial
      of Angela Davis. Some of the material has appeared else-
      where.

14   Armistead, Wilson A. A Tribute for the Negro. Connecticut:
      Irwin Manchester, 1848.
          Brief mention of several Black women in America and Africa
      including Phillis Wheatley, Nancy Pitchford, Rosetta, and
      Eva Bartels.

15   Atkinson, J. Edward. Black Dimensions in Contemporary Amer-
      ican Art. New York: New American Library, 1971.
          Several Black women artists and their works are included
      in this collection of artists: Margaret Burroughs, Mary
      Reed Daniel, Eugenia V. Dunn, Juette Johnson Day, Barbara
      J. Jones, Lois Mailou Jones, Delilah W. Pierce, Lucille
      Roberts, Nancy Rowland, Jewell Woodward; and Simon and Alma
      W. Thomas. Each artist's work follows her biographical
      sketch.

16   Bailey, Leaonead Pack. Broadside Authors and Artists: An
      Illustrated Biographical Directory. Detroit: Broadside
      Press, 1974.
          A biographical reference book of young and many older
      Black authors and artists of the Broadside Press. Many
      Black women's biographical sketches, as well as photos, are
      included in this needed work.

17   Bailey, Pearl. The Raw Pearl. New York: Harcourt, Brace
      and World, 1968.
          An autobiography of the Black entertainer, singer, and
      actress. Miss Bailey writes about her early childhood and
      the people who had a major influence on her later life,
      including her father who was a minister. Focuses mainly on
      her adult life as an entertainer as well as her philosophy
      of life.

18   _____. Talking to Myself. New York: Harcourt, Brace and
      World, 1971.

(Bailey, Pearl)
    Gives opinions on a variety of topics including the American family, the state of the nation, the conflict between the different age groups, the entertainment world as well as the price of fame and fortune. Also writes about birth, love, hate, and death. Her early religious upbringing is seen throughout the book. This is in a larger sense her other autobiography.

19   _____. Pearl's Kitchen: An Extraordinary Cookbook. New York: Harcourt, Brace, Jovanovich, 1972.
    Although many recipes are discussed, an insight is also given into the author's early life in Philadelphia, where she learned to cook from her mother. Also gives her opinions on: education, good manners, children, home, family life, friends, and some of the many countries and places she has visited over the years.

20   Barlow, Leila Mae. Across the Years, Memoirs. Montgomery: Paragon, 1959.
    The memoirs of a Black woman who taught in a Black American college. Tells of her personal philosophy and desires to strive towards excellence for herself and her students. Written in a simple direct prose style.

21   Baskin, Wade and Runes, Richard N. Dictionary of Black Culture. New York: Philosophical Library, 1973.
    A collection of short biographical sketches of women and men as well as events, movements, and organizations. There are more than 160 biographical sketches of Black women. There are no references or Index.

22   Bass, Charlotta A. Forty Years, Memoirs from the Pages of a Newspaper. Los Angeles: N. P., 1960.
    The author is a newspaper woman in Los Angeles, California. She tells of her many experiences while working on a Black newspaper, the "California Eagle," as editor and publisher for over forty years.

23   Bates, Daisy. The Long Shadow of Little Rock: A Memoir. New York: McKay, 1962.
    An autobiography of a Black woman born in Arkansas in the 1920's who led the fight for the integration of schools in Little Rock, Arkansas in 1957. She discusses her life in that southern state and all of the humiliations she encountered while she was a child. She has received the highest award of the NAACP--the Springarn Medal.

24   Beam, Lura. He Called Them by Lighting: A Teacher's Odyssey in the Negro South 1908-1919. New York: Bobbs-Merrill Co., 1969.

(Beam, Lura)
   Tells of a white woman sent to teach in the South in the
1920's by the American Missionary Association. She writes
of her observations as a teacher of Black children, citing
many concepts of how Black girls saw themselves and their
attitudes toward society. Also mentions the role of prominent Black women in the United States in the early twentieth century.

25   Bernard, Jacqueline. Journey Toward Freedom: The Story of
   Sojourner Truth. New York: Dell Publishing Co., 1967.
      Several topics on the Black woman are covered: "Women
   under Slavery," "The Unnatural Superiority of Negro Women,"
   "The Many Roles of (Black) Wives," "The Slave Mother," "The
   Mother Among Freedmen." A number of charts are included.

26   Berry, Pike. Birthed into Glory. Boston: Christopher, 1966.
      A biographic story, not a biography. It deals affection-
   ately with "colored nannys" particularly with the author's
   own--Mary--who lived with his family from 1900. The author
   is a southern born and educated lawyer who brings to light
   many humorous and enchanting events which have so far
   received little light in Black literature.

27   Billingsley, Andrew. Black Families in White America.
   Englewood Cliffs, New Jersey: Prentice-Hall, 1968.
      Many references to the role of the Black woman in the
   Black family are included. Gives a historical background
   of the Black family and the part the Black woman played in
   it throughout history.

28   Billington, Ray Allen, Editor. The Journal of Charlotte
   Forten: A Free Negro in the Slave Era. New York: Crowell-
   Collier, 1961.
      A record of the inner thoughts of a Black woman who became
   a teacher and whose race determined her attitude toward her
   fellow man, country, and even God. Her environment and
   background were factors that led her to dedicate her life
   to the cause of decency and freedom for Black people in the
   1800's. Covers the years between 1854-1864.

29   Blake, Jane. Memoirs of Margaret Jane Blake, Related to
   Sarah R. Levering, Baltimore, Whose Father Owned Jane Blake.
   Philadelphia: Innes and Son, 1897.
      The author was a slave in Baltimore, but was freed before
   the Civil War. She discusses her experiences under slavery
   and points out that slavery was more harmful to the slave-
   holder and their families than to the slaves.

30   Blesh, Rudi. Combo: U. S. A.: Eight Lives in Jazz. Philadelphia: Chilton Book Co., 1970.

(Blesh, Rudi)
    This compilation of Black musicians' biographies contains men exclusively except for Eleanora Gough Fagan, better known as Billie Holiday and affectionately called "Lady Day." Contains excellent discography and index. There are several photos of Miss Holiday.

31   Bontemps, Arna. <u>Great Slave Narratives</u>. Boston: Beacon Press, 1969.
    A collection of three slave narratives including "Running a Thousand Miles for Freedom." or, "The Escape of William and Ellen Craft from Slavery." This is one slave narrative that sees a Black woman, even though she could pass for white, working side by side with her husband to gain freedom. The Crafts also published their narratives in 1860. This is one of the most unusual narratives ever written.

32   Botkin, B. A., Editor. <u>Lay My Burden Down: A Folk History of Slavery</u>. Chicago: University of Chicago Press, 1945.
    A collection of excerpts and narratives from the Slave Narrative Collection of 1944 Federal Writers' Project. Many are from Black women who had been ex-slaves or whose parents were former slaves.

33   Bothume, Elizabeth Hyde. <u>First Days Amongst the Contrabands</u>. Boston: Lee and Shepard, 1893.
    Miss Bothume was a white teacher from New York who went to South Carolina to help teach ex-slaves. Here she discusses the conditions of the freedman when she went South. A number of Black ex-slave women voices are quoted throughout this work. While in the South the writer learned to appreciate the Black woman's common sense approach to problems.

34   Boulware, Marcus H. <u>The Oratory of Negro Leaders: 1900-1968</u>. Westport, Connecticut: Negro Universities Press, 1969.
    Includes the "Public Addresses of Negro Women." Some of the Black women listed are well known: Charlotte Hawkins Brown, Mary McLeod Bethune, Mary Church Terrell, etc. Also mentions the oration of lesser known Black women: Lillian Wheeler Smith, Laura Croslry, Carolina Johnson, Dorothy Ferefee, Belle Hendon, etc.

35   Bradford, Sarah Elizabeth. <u>Harriett: The Moses of Her People</u>. Reprint of the 1886 edition. New York: Corinth Books, 1961.
    A biography of a Black woman who was one of the leaders of the Underground Railroad. Gives a detailed account of her early life but tells us little about her life after the Civil War when she moved back to New York. There a few appendix letters but no documentation, bibliography, or footnotes.

36   Branch, Essie. <u>My Name is Arnold</u>. Chicago: DuSable Museum
      of Negro History, 1971.
          A composite of many childrens' conversations for the con-
      struction of one Black family. Various references are made
      to the mother throughout the book. The Black families in
      this book were living in Chicago in a housing project.

37   Brawley, Benjamin Griffith. <u>Women of Achievement</u>. Chicago:
      Women's American Baptist Home Mission Society, 1919.
          A collection of short biographies and sketches of the fol-
      lowing Black women: Harriet Tubman, Nora Gordon, Meta
      Warrich Fuller, Mary McLeod Bethune, and Mary Church
      Terrell. Also an introduction chapter "The Negro Woman in
      American Life." Photographs of each woman are included.

38   _____. <u>Negro Builders and Heroes</u>. Chapel Hill: University
      of North Carolina Press, 1937.
          Several chapters on Black women: "The Negro Woman in
      American Life," "Women Who Have Led in Education," "Maggie
      L. Walker and Her Enterprise," "Phillis Wheatley," "Harriet
      Tubman and Her Underground Railroad," and "Sojourner."
      Emphasizes the point that "In the history of the United
      States no more heroic work has been done than that performed
      by the Negro Woman."

39   _____. <u>The Negro Genius</u>. New York: Dodd, Mead and Co.,
      1937.
          Several Black women and their works are discussed:
      Phillis Wheatley, Elizabeth Taylor Greenfield, Frances E.
      W. Harper, The Hyers Sisters, Madame Marie Selika, Flora
      Batson Bergen, Sissieretta Jones, Meta Warrick Fuller, Alice
      Dunbar, Zora Neale Hurston, Rose McClendon, and Marian
      Anderson. A short biographical sketch on each is included.

40   Brehan, Delle. <u>Kicks is Kicks</u>. Los Angeles: Holloway
      House, 1970.
          A detailed account of the author as a "woman of pleasure"
      while living in New York during the 1950's. She was some-
      times called the "Black Queen of Pain." Also describes how
      she became mentally prepared for her "vocation."

41   Brooks, Gwendolyn. <u>Report from Part One</u>. Detroit: Broadside
      Press, 1972.
          An autobiographical work by Gwendolyn Brooks, the first
      Black (man or woman) to win a Pulitzer Prize. Tells of her
      family background, girlhood, marriage, children, and her
      journey to Africa. Photos of the author, her family, and
      friends, are included. Also three interviews with the
      writer as well as two appendices.

42   Broughton, Virginia W. Twenty's Experience of a Missionary.
      Chicago: Pony Press, 1907.
          The author writes about her experiences not only as a
      missionary, but also as a teacher and principal in Tennes-
      see. Miss Broughton was born free in Virginia in the 1800s
      and graduated from Fisk University in 1875. Somewhat hard
      to follow at times because it is written in the third per-
      son.

43   Brown, Charlotte Hawkins. The Correct Things to Do, to Say,
      to Wear. Boston: Christopher Publishing House, 1941.
          A Black educator writes of her years of experience and
      observation of social grace. She discusses definite prin-
      ciples upon which charm depend. She was called "The First
      Lady of Social Graces."

44   Brown, Hallie Quinn, Editor. Homespun Heroines and Women of
      Distinction. Xenia, Ohio: Aldrine Publishing Co., 1926.
          A collection of sketches and brief biographies of fifty-
      five Black women throughout history from Martha Payne, moth-
      er of Daniel A. Payne, founder of Wilberforce University, to
      "Aunt Mac," and Eliza P. Fox, President of the Woman's Bap-
      tist Association of Virginia. Many photos of the women are
      included. One of the best early books on Black women.

45   Brown, Jane. Narratives of Jane Brown and Her Two Children.,
      Related to the Reverend G. W. Offey. Hartford: G. W.
      Offey, 1860.
          Another slave narrative by a woman slave.

46   Brown, Julia Clarice. I Testify: My Years as an Undercover
      Agent for the F. B. I. Belmont, California: Western
      Islands, 1966.
          The autobiography of a Black woman who served as a confi-
      dential agent for the F.B.I. between 1951 and 1960. Mrs.
      Brown had successfully penetrated some of the most secret
      and sensitive segments of the communist network in the
      United States. Mostly about her relationship with the Com-
      munist Party and how she was constantly in danger by giving
      her information to the F.B.I. Reveals the continuing pat-
      tern of Communist warfare in the United States.

47   Brown, Sterling. Negro Poetry and Drama and the Negro in
      American Fiction. Reprint of the 1937 edition. New York:
      Atheneuni, 1969.
          Several Black women and their works are discussed in this
      book: Phillis Wheatley, Georgia Douglas Johnson, Alice
      Dunbar Nelson, Anne Spencer, Jessie Fauset, etc. Also a
      short biographical sketch of each woman.

48   Brown, Williams Wells. Clotelle; or the Colored Heroine, A
      Tale of the Southern States. Reprint of the 1867 edition

(Brown, Williams Wells)
    published by Lee and Shepard, Boston. Miami, Florida:
Mnemosyne Publishing Co., 1969.
    Historical novel written much like reality portrays the
South as it was just prior to the end of the Civil War.
Clotelle, a Black woman slave, of mixed-blood exemplified
the tragedies and the triumphs of both races of that era.

49   Browne, Mattie Griffiths. Autobiography of a Female Slave.
    New York: Redfield, 1857.
        A rare autobiography of a Black female slave. The author
not only writes about her childhood under slavery but the
cruelties of the system as well as the different attitudes
of her several owners. The author was freed and given a
sum of four thousand dollars by her last owner. The will
bequested that she would live somewhere in the North, which
she did. The author later taught a small school of Black
children in a small town in Massachusetts.

50   Browne, Rose Butler. Love My Children: An Autobiography.
    New York: Meredith Press, 1962.
        A sympathetic autobiography of a Black woman's dedication
to education and racial betterment. Her goal for a Harvard
Ph.D. was a united effort of her family and their purpose
for racial advancement. Beginning in humble origins in
Boston, the author carries the reader through an educational odyssey terminating at North Carolina College.

51   Brownmiller, Susan. Shirley Chisholm: A Biography. New
    York: Doubleday and Co., 1971.
        A biography of the major events in Mrs. Chisholm's life
and career from her childhood in Barbados and Brooklyn
through her election as the first Black Congresswoman. Like
most biographies it includes many people, past and present,
who influenced Mrs. Chisholm. Includes a number of photographs, most of which have appeared elsewhere. Especially
good for young people.

52   Bruce, John Edward. Short Biographical Sketches of Eminent
    Negro Men and Women in Europe and the United States.
    Yonkers, New York: Gazette Press, 1910.
        This is Volume 1 of a multi-volume set. Written in the
style of a high school textbook complete with questions following each biographical sketch. No table of contents or
index. Not even strictly alphabetical in arrangement. Contains only two sketches on women: Ida B. Wells, a jour-
nalist, and Phillis Wheatley, the Poet.

53   Bruyn, Kathlee. "Aunt" Clara Brown: Story of a Black Pio-
    neer. Boulder, Colorado: Pruett Publishing Co., 1970.

(Bruyn, Kathlee)

The biography of a Black woman slave in Kentucky who
gained her freedom and later migrated to Colorado and became an outstanding pioneer in that state. Written as a
tribute to Clara Brown. There are several photos of Miss
Brown and other Blacks. Footnotes follow each chapter as
well as a complete bibliography.

54   Bryant, Emmie Lee. A Thousand Victories for a Black Woman.
Los Angeles, California: Emmie Lee Bryant, 1968.

Intended to encourage and inspire everyone to the aware-
ness and the knowledge of his Maker (God). Contains many
proverbs, as well as chapters on various aspects of the
Bible. The author is a deeply religious woman and reflects
her christian teaching and upbringing in her writings.

55   Buckmater, Henrietta. Let My People Go. New York: Harper
and Brothers, 1941.

A history of the anti-slavery movement in the United
States and the role of the Underground Railroad. Also mentions the part that Black women and men played in it.
Harriet Tubman was one of the most heroic figure conductors
in the Underground Railroad. Yet the author minimizes her
contributions.

56   _____. Women Who Shaped History. New York: Coules, 1958.

Brief sketches of six American women whose outstanding
leadership and influence help shape history. One Black woman is also included among the six: Harriet Tubman, leader
in Civil Rights and advocate of human dignity.

57   Burt, Olive W. Negroes in the Early West. New York: Julian
Messner, 1969.

Includes biographical sketches of Black women. The chapter on women discusses: "Mammy Pleasant" who owned a boarding house and eating establishment in San Francisco in the
1870s and 1890s. She became very rich and was a friend of
John Brown. Biddy Mason was a former slave in Missouri who
later married and settled in Los Angeles, where she and her
husband owned a successful store and were wealthy. Mary
Fields or "Black Mary" was a servant, restaurant keeper,
stage driver, washer-woman, and baby-sitter. She was born a
slave in Tennessee about 1832 and escaped to Ohio and then
to Montana. Mary died in 1914, eighty-two years old in
Cascade, Montana. Written for young people.

58   Burton, Annie L. Memories of Childhood Slavery Days. Boston:
Ross Publishing Co., 1909.

An account of slavery in the United States as it comes to
its end, as seen through the eyes of a child. Describes the
life styles and feelings of slavery as well as the dehumanization of the institution of that system. Shows the

(Burton, Annie L.)
    different life styles of Northern Blacks and Southern
    Blacks. There are also some poems and religious hymns in
    this book.

59   Cade, Toni. The Black Woman: An Anthology. New York:
     Signet, 1970.
        A collection of writings on Black women by Black men and
     women. Several poems about Black women are also included.
     A wide range of topics are included: "Motherhood," "Who
     Will Revere the Black Woman?" "Double Jeopardy: To Be
     Black and Female," "On the Issue of Roles," "Ebony Minds,
     Black Voices," etc.

60   Campbell, Marie. Folks Do Get Born. New York: Rinehart &
     Co., 1946.
        Examines Black midwives in Georgia and other southern
     states, and points out the important services that the mid-
     wives render in rural areas. In the 1930s, they delivered
     about forty-two percent of the babies in rural Georgia.
     When the State Board of Health of Georgia first assumed re-
     sponsibility for supervising and licensing midwives, in 1925,
     there were approximately 9,000 practicing in Georgia. Black
     midwives were at one time on the State Board. Also dis-
     cusses the midwife clubs, meetings and views on life.

61   Carson, Josephine. Silent Voices: The Southern Negro Woman
     Today. New York: Delacorte Press, 1969.
        The work is an impression and the search for a silenced
     voice, the Black woman, almost invisible in the United
     States. The Black author discusses the historical role that
     Black women have played and the double restrictions she fac-
     es: She is a woman and Black. A brief list of "firsts" for
     Black women are also included at the end of the books.

62   Carruth, Ella Kaiser. She Wanted to Read: The Story of Mary
     McLeod Bethune. Nashville and New York: Abingdon Press,
     1966.
        The title tells the essence of this short, 80 page, biog-
     raphy of this great educator. Written especially for young
     people. The author devotes over half of the book to Mrs.
     Bethune's childhood. The other half of this work discusses
     the accomplishment of the biographee during her adult life
     including the founding of Bethune-Cookman College, and The
     National Council of Negro Women.

63   Cherry, Gwendolyn, et. al. Portraits in Color: The Lives of
     Colorful Negro Women. New York: Pageant Press, 1962.
        A collection of biographies of contemporary Black American
     women from a variety of fields: Education, Music, Enter-
     tainment, Sports, Business, Literary and Civil Rights. Pho-
     tos and biographies of each woman are included.

64   Child, Lydia Maria. The Freemen's Book. Boston: Ticknor and
      Fields, 1865.
        A textbook used in the freemen's schools written by a
      white abolitionist. It includes essays, short biographies,
      poems, anecdotes, and household hints. Many of the works
      were by and about Black men and Black women. Works by Black
      women included those of Frances E. W. Harper, Phillis
      Wheatley, Harriet Jacobs and Charlotte L. Forten.

65   Chisholm, Shirley. Unbought and Unbossed. Boston: Houghton
      and Mifflin Co., 1970.
        The autobiography of the first Black woman elected to the
      U.S. House of Representatives in 1968. Mrs. Chisholm writes
      about her early childhood in Barbados and Brooklyn as well
      as her rise to elected office. She tells how she managed to
      combine a political life with a happy marriage. The author
      has shown how to bridge the gaps of generation, sex, and
      race.

66   _____. The Good Fight. New York: Harper and Row, 1973.
        The story of Shirley Chisholm's campaign for the United
      States presidency. It tells of her continuing struggle for
      the reform of American politics as well as commitment to the
      cause of equal justice for Black people and for women. The
      author tells the truth as she sees it regardless of its
      effect on her political future. Included in the Appendix is
      a speech on women, entitled, "Economic Justice for Women."

67   Clark, Septima with Le Gette Blyth. Echo in My Soul. New
      York: Dutton and Co., 1962.
        An autobiography by a former Black Southern school teacher
      who was born in the late 1890s. Discusses her early educa-
      tion and what life was like for Blacks in the South during
      her lifetime, a period of over fifty years. Tells of her
      efforts in getting equal salaries for Black teachers in the
      South.

68   Cole, Maria Ellington with Louis Robinson. Nat King Cole:
      An Intimate Biography. New York: Morrow and Co., 1971.
        Mrs. Cole gives an intimate glimpse into the private life
      of not only her husband, the famous entertainer, but also
      her relationship with him. Discusses her joy and sorrow
      during her marriage to the "King."

69   Conrad, Earl. Harriet Tubman: Negro Solder and Abolitionist.
      New York: International Press, 1968.
        A biography written for young people on the great Black
      abolitionist, Harriet Tubman, and her role and leadership in
      the Underground Railroad.

70   Cooper, Anna Julia. A Voice from the South by a Black
      Woman of the South. Xenia, Ohio: Aldrine Printing House,
      1892.

(Cooper, Anna Julia)
An autobiography of an ex-slave who acquired a college education, became an educator, and later a founder of a university. Many of her essays and speeches are included in the book. Emphasizes the important role of the Black woman in America.

71 Coppin, Fannie Jackson. Reminiscences of School Life, and Hints on Teaching. Philadelphia: African Methodist Episcopal Book Concern, 1913.
An autobiography of a Black woman born a slave who later gained her freedom, acquired a college degree in 1865 and became an educator of the Institute for Colored Youth and then principal of its Female Department. Mrs. Jackson introduced many innovations into the education system which were remarkable, especially for that time period.

72 Cotton, Ella Earls. A Spark for My People: The Sociological Autobiography of a Negro Teacher. New York: Exposition Press, 1954.
A moving autobiography of a Black woman who taught in the public schools in the Deep South for more than forty years. She re-creates the struggle for Black people for education in the South from the Reconstruction Era to present. Tells of the quiet heroism of dedicated Black teachers rising above their limited equipment, indifferences and hostilities of whites. Gives a brief sketch of her early life in Virginia and the people that influenced her later life.

73 Crummell, Alexander. Africa and America: Addresses and Discourses. Springfield, Mass.: Willey and Company, 1891.
Includes a discussion on the historical role of the Black woman in America and emphasizes "her neglects and her needs." Concludes that there are six things the Black women of the South need, among which are schools and education.

74 Culp, Daniel Wallace. Twentieth Century Negro Literature: Or a Cyclopedia of Thought on the Vital Topics Relating to the American Negro. Naperville, Illinois: Nichols, 1902.
Short biographical sketches of twelve Black women are included in the section, "What Role is the Educated Woman to Play in the Uplifting of her Race?" The women discussed are: Mrs. Areil S. Bowen, Mrs. Rosa D. Bowser, Mrs. Paul Lawrence Dunbar, Miss Lena A. Jackson, Mrs. Warren Logan, Mrs. Sarah Dudley Pettey, Mrs. M. E. C. Smith, Mrs. Rosetta Douglass Sprague, Mary B. Talbert, Mrs. Josephine Yates, Mrs. Lena Mason, and Mrs. Mary Church Terrell. Photos of the women are also included.

75 Cunard, Nancy. Negro Anthology. New York: Frederick Unger Publishing Co., 1970.

(Cunard, Nancy)

Several articles on and by Black women are included in this Black anthology by a white Englishwoman. First published in London, England, in 1934.

76   Cuthbert, Marion Vera. Education and Marginality: A Study of the Negro Woman College Graduate. New York: Columbia University Press, 1942.

A study of the effect of the college experience upon lives of a number of Black women. Dr. Cuthbert indicates what seems to be the more satisfactory adjustments to be made and compensations to be gained during this period of emergence by a significant group of Black women with a college education. Gives some psychological and sociological implications for educated Black women and some of the problems in life that they encounter because of their educational background.

77   Dabney, Wendell Phillip. Maggie L. Walker and the I. O. Saint Luke: The Woman and Her Work. Cincinnati, Ohio: Danbey, 1927.

A biography of a Black woman born in Richmond, Virginia in the mid-1800s who rose to become founder and President of the Saint Luke Bank and Trust Company (stated as being the oldest Black banking institution in America). Even though the work discusses her early childhood, most of it is devoted to her adult life. Several photos are included in the book as well as a number of testimonial speeches about Mrs. Walker.

78   Dandridge, Dorothy and Conrad, Earl. Everything and Nothing: The Dorothy Dandridge Tragedy. New York: Abelard-Schuman Limited, 1970.

The autobiography of the famous actress Dorothy Dandridge. Miss Dandridge writes of her early childhood in Cleveland and the influence of her mother on her and her sister. Tells of her many crises and how she overcame them. The writer makes the point that "the problem in America is not exactly race, but racism, which is hatred." There are several photos of the actress. Miss Dandridge died in 1965 at the age of 42.

79   Daniel, Sadie Iola. Woman Builders. Washington, D.C.: The Associated Publisher, 1931.

The stories of seven Black women who contributed to the development of Black children in the United States through educational and social institutions that they established. The women are: Lucy Craft Laney, Maggie Lena Walker, Janie Porter Barnett, Mary McLeod Bethune, Nannie Helen Burroughs, Charlotte Hawkins Brown, and Jane Edna Hunter. Photographs of the women are included.

14

80 Dann, Martin E. The Black Press, 1827-1890: The Quest for
    National Identity. New York: G. P. Putnam's Sons, 1971.
      Nine portraits and sketches of Black women journalists
    during the 1880s: Mrs. N. F. Mossell, Mrs. Lucretio Newman
    Coleman, Miss Ida B. Wells, Mrs. W. E. Mathews, Miss Mary
    Cook, Lillial Akbeeta Kewius, Mrs. Amelia F. Johnson, Miss
    Mary E. Britton, Miss Ione E. Wood, and Miss Kate D.
    Chapman. A list of eighteen other Black women who did spe-
    cial work and contributed valuable articles to weekly and
    monthly publications is included.

81 Dannett, Sylvia. Profile of Negro Womanhood. Westport,
    Conn.: Negro Universities Press, 1964.
      Brief biographies and sketches of Black women in the Fine
    Arts, Education, Medicine, Law, Nursing, Performing Arts,
    Social Work, Literary, Civil Rights, and Government. Notes
    and a comprehensive bibliography are included.

82 Davenport, M. Marguerite. Azalia: The Life of Madame E.
    Azalia Hackley. Boston: Chapman and Grimes, Inc., 1947.
      A biography of a Black woman born in 1867 who later became
    one of America's outstanding pioneers in the field of seri-
    ous music. She reached her apogee at the dawn of the twen-
    tieth century. Sees Miss Hackley as a great artist,
    lecturer, missionary, and even philanthropist. There is
    also a "Chronological Table of Significant Events in the
    Life of Azalia," at the end.

83 Davis, Angela. Angela Davis: An Autobiography. New York:
    Random House, 1974.
      The first full length autobiography by Angela Davis. It
    is an account of her childhood, youth and growth, and her
    conversion to Communism. Gives the reader a new insight
    into Blacks and radical political movements of the 1960s.
    Many of Miss Davis' discussions have political overtones,
    and this autobiography should be read with that in mind.

84 Davis, Angela and Aptheker, Bettina. If They Come in the
    Morning: Voices of Resistance. New York: The Third Press,
    1971.
      A collection of essays, letters, poetry, and articles by
    Miss Davis, Ruchell Magee, the three Soledad Brothers, and
    others. There is a political biography of Angela Davis as
    well as "A Call to Black Women of Every Religious and Polit-
    ical Persuasion." Also included are statements and appeals
    on Miss Davis' behalf by Coretta King and Shirley Graham
    DuBois.

85 Davis, Elizabeth L. Lifting as They Climb: The National
    Association of Colored Women. Washington, D.C.,: The
    National Association of Colored Women, 1933.

(Davis, Elizabeth L.)
An Historical Record of the National Association of Colored Women and other items of interest. There are several biographical sketches of many Black women in that organization. Discusses the role of the Black woman in various vocations in several states. Several photos of many of the members of the organization are also included.

86 Davis, John P., Editor. The American Negro Reference Book. Englewood Cliff, New Jersey: Prentice-Hall, 1966.
There is a section in this work on the American Black woman. It includes: "Sex and Age Distribution," "Negro Women in the Labor Force," "Occupational Distribution," "The College Educated Negro Women," "Marriage and Family Life," "Negro Women's Organization," and "Negro Women in Civil Rights Struggles."

87 Day, Beth. Sexual Life Between Blacks and Whites: The Roots of Racism. New York: World Publishing Co., 1972.
About a third of this book is devoted to the past and present role of the Black woman. Miss Day relates to the historical position of the Black woman from slavery to the present. One of the most interesting chapters is "Black Liberation and Women's Liberation."

88 Day, Helen Caldwell. Color, Ebony. New York: Sheed and Ward, 1951.
An autobiography by a Black woman about her experiences and her sudden realization that some whites can be human. Writes about her family and the many inequalities forced on educated Blacks. She also discusses the Catholic Church and her opinion of it. Written when the author was only 23 years old. She discusses race relations in the United States as well as the excellent work that the Catholic Church is doing, especially in Memphis and the South.

89 _____. Not Without Tears. New York: Sheed and Ward, 1954.
The author continues her autobiography that was published in 1951. She writes of her beliefs in racial justice and human cooperation and understanding.

90 Delaney, Lucy A. Berry. From Darkness Cometh the Light. St. Louis, Mo.: J. T. Smith Publishing House, 1891.
A moving autobiography of the author from her childhood to young adulthood. Discusses how her mother, a free-born Black, had been kidnapped and sold into slavery and how she was also sold into slavery. The author acquired her freedom after a long hard struggle in jail for her legal battle for freedom. This work shows the determination of a Black woman to fight against the incredible odds to obtain her freedom.

91   Dobler, Lavinia Grand and Toppin, Edgar A. Pioneers and
     Patriots: The Lives of Six Negroes of the Revolutionary
     Era. New York: Doubleday, 1965.
          Of the six Blacks discussed, over twenty pages are
     devoted to Phillis Wheatley. This was one of a number of
     books written for children and young people.

92   Douty, Esther M. Charlotte Forten: Free Black Teacher.
     Champaign, Illinois: Garrard Publishing Co., 1971.
          An intimate biography of the great Black teacher, author,
     and fighter for the abolition of slavery. Written by a
     white woman for children and young people. Focuses on Miss
     Forten's career as a teacher. Much of this material is
     based on the original unpublished Journal of Miss Forten.
     There are a number of photos and illustrations included in
     this work.

93   DuBois, W. E. B. Darkwater. New York: Shocken Books, 1969.
          Included is a discussion of four women the author remem-
     bers from his childhood: his mother, cousin Inez, Emma, and
     Ida Fuller. They represent the problems of the widow, the
     wife, the maiden, and the outcast. Examines the roles Black
     women have played throughout history and the message they
     have for America and the world.

94   _____. The Philadelphia Negro: A Social Study: Together
     with a Special Report on Domestic Service by Isabel Eaton.
     New York: Schocken Books, 1967.
          There are mentions of the Black women in Philadelphia and
     their relationships to the family, education, religion, etc.
     The section of "Special Report on Negro Domestic Service"
     discusses in detail the role of Black women in domestic ser-
     vices, in which over 91 percent of Black women of Pennsyl-
     vania were engaged.

95   Dunham, Katherine. A Touch of Innocence. New York:
     Harcourt, Brace and Co., 1959.
          The autobiographical narrative of a Black woman born in
     Chicago in 1910 and who later became a world famous dancer
     and choreographer. Miss Dunham writes of childhood and the
     people who influenced her early life. Unlike other works
     of this kind, this book is history, because it deals with
     people of different racial backgrounds. The author, how-
     ever, only writes about the first eighteen years of her
     life.

96   _____. Katherine Dunham's Journey to Accompong. New York:
     Henry Holt and Co., 1946.
          An account of Miss Dunham's experience in Accompong,
     Jamaica, while on an anthropological field trip to the West
     Indies undertaken on a Julius Rosenwald Travel Fellowship.

(Dunham, Katherine)
Provides an insight into her often overlooked role as an
anthropologist.

97 _____. Island Possessed. Garden City, New York: Doubleday
and Co., 1969.
Miss Dunham writes of her experience in Haiti which she
considers her spiritual home. While in Haiti in 1936 on a
Rosenwald Travel Fellowship to study "primitive" dance and
ritual, the writer learned of the history and politics of
the country in the early days of its independence. She also
met many of the leaders of the country and developed a deep
and abiding affection of all the people she met there.

98 Dunnigan, Alice Allison. A Black Woman's Experience: From
Schoolhouse to White House. Philadelphia: Dorrance & Co.,
1974.
One of the latest autobiographies by a Black woman.
Writes of her early childhood in Kentucky and many years of
teaching in the Kentucky schools before being employed by
the Federal Government as an economist. Mrs. Dunnigan was
later appointed under the Kennedy Administration as Educational Consultant to the President's Committee on Equal
Employment Opportunity. She was the first Black woman to
hold that key position. The author also was a newspaper
woman for many years.

99 Duster, Alfreda, M., Editor. Crusade for Justice: The Autobiography of Ida B. Wells. Chicago: University of Chicago
Press, 1970.
The autobiography of a Black woman who fought lynching
and other forms of barbarianism almost single-handed, at a
time when few men or women dared to speak out. Tells of her
private life as well as public works. She writes about a
number of events in her life: caring for her family, trying
to develop Black leadership, serving as a correspondent for
a big city newspaper without compromising principles.
Edited by her daughter, Mrs. Alfreda M. Duster. An index,
bibliography, and photos of Miss Wells and her family are
included. Miss Wells died in 1931.

100 Edmonds, Helen G. Black Faces in High Places: Negroes in
Government. New York: Harcourt, 1971.
A discussion of Black office-holders in the Legislative,
Judicial, and Executive Branches of Government in the United
States including Black women office-holders. Black women
are also discussed at the state and local levels.

101 Eldridge, Elleanore. Memoirs of Elleanore Eldridge: Woman of
Colour. Reprint of the 1842 edition published by B. T.
Alboro. Austin and New York: The Pemberton Press, 1969.
An early narrative written by a Black woman. Elleanore
Eldridge was born a slave on March 26, 1785 in Warwick,

(Eldridge, Elleanore)
Rhode Island, and later bought her freedom from her owner.
Over the years Miss Eldridge had acquired some property,
which was taken from her because of alleged back taxes,
which she was not aware of. The main purpose of this small
book was to tell her story of the unjust sale of her property and also to use the money from the sale of this book to
try to get her property back. These "Memoirs" were written
in the second person, and are explained by an unknown white
woman.

102   Epstein, Sam and Epstein, Beryl. Harriet Tubman: Guide to
Freedom. New York: Garrard, 1968.
    Biography of the great abolitionist and Underground Rail-
road leader written for high school students and young
adults. Much of the material has been published in other
books.

103   Evans, Mari. I Am a Black Woman. New York: Morrow, 1970.
    A collection of eighty poems by a Black woman. They are
lyrical and penetrating, dealing with love, loneliness,
children, and Blackness. In this book she is magnifying her
life and experiences as a Black woman. Several photos are
included in the book.

104   Everett, Syble Ethel Byrd. Adventures With Life: An Autobiography of a Distinguished Negro Citizen. Boston: Meador
Publishing Co., 1945.
    An autobiography of a Black woman who was born in Okla-
homa at the turn of the twentieth century and later became
a teacher in the same state. Tells of her educational experiences while attending the University of Utah. The author
was very active in church work and her Christian background
can be seen throughout the book. There are also several
poems by the writer included.

105   Evers, Mrs. Medgar. For Us the Living. Garden City, New
York: Doubleday, 1967.
    An autobiography by the wife of the slain Civil Rights
leader Medgar Evers. She discusses not only her husband's
work, but also tells the story of her early life and of her
marriage. The author mentions her modest role in the movement for human justice that she shared with her husband.

106   Fausett, Arther H. Sojourner Truth: God's Faithful Pilgrim.
New York: Russell & Russell, 1971.
    A biography of the great Black abolitionist and religious
leader written in narrative form.

107   Fax, Elton C. Contemporary Black Leaders. New York: Dodd,
Mead and Co., 1969.

(Fax, Elton C.)
Of the fourteen individuals written about, three are
women: Coretta Scott King, Fannie Lou Hammer, and Ruby Dee.
The author gives a 17 page biographical sketch of each.

108   _____. Seventeen Black Artists. New York: Dodd, Mead & Co.,
1971.
Three Black women artists are included in this work:
Elizabeth Catlett, Charlotte Amevor, and Norma Morgan.
Miss Catlett was born in the United States but now lives in
Mexico. Miss Amevor was also born in America, traveled to
Africa, and bases most of her paintings on personal experi-
ences. Miss Morgan was born in America, traveled and stud-
ied in England, regards herself as a modern romantic artist.
There are photos of the artists, as well as some illustra-
tions of their works.

109 Feldstein, Stanley. Once a Slave: The Slaves' View of Slavery. New York: William Morrow and Co., 1971.
There are many references by and about Black women as
slaves as well as free women. Cites many autobiographies of
Black women. Includes an excellent bibliography.

110 Ferris, Louanne. I'm Done Crying. New York: New American
Library, 1969.
An autobiographical work by a Southern Black girl who
moved North and became a nurse. Miss Ferris discusses what
goes on in a poorly run hospital. The portrait she paints
in one of brutality, degradation, indifference, and corrup-
tion.

111 Finke, Blythe Foote. Angela Davis: Traitor or Martyr of the
Freedom of Expression. Charlotteville, New York: Sam Har
Press, 1972.
A short book--25 pages--about the Black "revolutionary
Marxist scholar," Angela Yvonne Davis. Most of the informa-
tion in this book was taken from Miss Davis' speeches and
other periodicals and magazines. Very little is new and it
adds little to our understanding of Miss Davis.

112 Fleming, Alice. Great Women Teachers. Philadelphia: J. B.
Lippincott Co., 1965.
A collection of life stories of ten pioneering women edu-
cators in the United States from the nineteenth century to
present. Of the ten discussed, one is a Black woman--Mary
McLeod Bethune, In the 14 page biographical sketch of her,
the author tells how Miss Bethune left the cotton fields of
South Carolina in the early 1900s and eventually created the
Bethune Cookman College in 1904 with only $1.50 in her
pocket.

113 Foote, Julia. <u>A Brand Plucked from the Fire: An Autobio-
     graphical Sketch</u>. Cleveland: W. F. Schneider Publisher,
     1879.
       The author discusses her evangelistic work and how it
     affected her life. She stresses the need for religious
     uplifting for her people.

114 Frazier, E. Franklin. <u>The Negro Family in the United States</u>.
     Reprint of the 1939 edition. Chicago: University of
     Chicago Press, 1966.
       Includes a discussion on the different roles played by a
     grandmother in the Black community and a grandmother in the
     white community. The Black grandmother more often assumes
     the role as head of household and has a major influence on
     the lives of the members of her family.

115 _____. <u>Black Bourgeoisie</u>. New York: The Free Press, 1957.
       One section tells of some Black women who avoid identify-
     ing with most Blacks and seek social status and acceptance
     through emulation of white society.

116 Gaines, Ernest J. <u>The Autobiography of Miss Jane Pittman</u>.
     New York: Dial Press, 1971.
       A novel based on the real life character of a Black woman
     who lived to be 110 years old. Tells of her life in slavery
     and her struggle for freedom. Shows a wise woman and her
     insights into the human conditions of mankind. Miss Pitt-
     man's opinion of other Black women during her life time are
     discussed.

117 Gayle, Addison, Jr. <u>Black Expression: Essays By and About
     Black Americans in the Creative Arts</u>. New York: Weybright
     and Talley, 1969.
       Several Black women and their works are included in this
     book: Margaret Walker, Toni Cade, Sarah Webster Fabio,
     Jessie Fauset, and Barbara Christian. There are also var-
     ious references to Black throughout most of the essays.

118 Gibson, Althea. <u>I Always Wanted to Be Somebody</u>. New York:
     Harper and Row, 1958.
       The autobiography of a Black woman born in the South,
     raised in Harlem and her struggle to gain success as an
     international tennis player. She tells of her childhood
     experiences and how they helped to influence her later life.

119 _____. <u>So Much to Live For</u>. New York: Putnam, 1968.
       This work is a continuation of her earlier autobiography.
     Miss Gibson writes about her life after she retired from
     tennis and became a professional golfer. She mentions the
     many adjustments that she had to make as a Black woman and
     an athlete.

120 Gilbert, Mercedes. <u>Aunt Sara's Wooden God</u>. Reprint of the
1938 edition published by The Christopher Publishing House,
New York. College Park, Maryland: McGrath Publishing Co.,
1972.
A novel written by one of America's leading Black actresses. This is an authentic story of thousands of poor Blacks
living in the South. The "Wooden God" in this work is a
mulatto country boy, worshipped by his mother, but unable to
fulfill the faith that his mother has in him because of poverty and prejudice. The ironic tragedy portrays Blacks in
the South.

121 Giovanni, Nikki. <u>Gemini: An Extended Autobiographical State-
ment on My First Twenty-Five Years of Being a Black Poet</u>.
New York: Bobbs-Merrill, 1972.
The title tells what the book is about. The author tells
about her early life and the people who influenced her.
There are several photographs of Miss Giovanni and her
family.

122 _____, Editor. <u>Night Comes Softly</u>. New York: Medic Press,
1970.
Many authors contributed to this anthology edited by
Giovanni, which accounts for its uneven texture. The glue
holding this work together is the Blackness and feminism of
the authors. The nature of the poems is generally painful.
The bibliography, however, is excellent and contains bio-
graphic data on many of the contributing poets.

123 Goodwin, Ruby Berkley. <u>It's Good to be Black</u>. Garden City,
New York: Doubleday and Company, Inc., 1953.
The autobiography of a Black woman who was raised in Du
Quoin, Illinois. Discusses her early childhood and the
impact that her family had on her upbringing. The writer
had a happy childhood in Du Quoin, and stated that her frustrations based on color did not come in childhood, but in
maturity, after she left her father's house and the friendly
little town of Du Quoin.

124 Graddings, Paula, Editor. <u>A Poetic Equation: Conversations
Between Nikki Giovanni and Margaret Walker</u>. Washington,
D.C.: Howard University Press, 1974.
Two outstanding poets give a variety of opinions on a num-
ber of topics. The chapters include: "Two Views: One Des-
tiny," "Violence and the Decision to Respond," "Content and
Intent: Some Thoughts on Writing," "Criticism and Film,"
"Notebook," "The Last War," and "In/Conclusion." The book
was based on 500 pages of transcript, and took place in
November, 1972 and January, 1973. There are also more than
50 snapshots of the poets.

125   Graham, Shirley. The Story of Phillis Wheatley. New York:
       Messner, 1949.
           A biography for young people about the first recognized
       Black woman poet in America. More than just the story of a
       Black girl in colonial America, it tells of the epoch of
       slavery and the rise of individual Blacks seeking to escape
       the burdens of it. Many of Miss Wheatley's poems are in-
       cluded in this book.

126   Greenfield, Eloise. Rosa Parks. New York: Thomas Y. Crowell
       Company, 1973.
           A short biography, 32 pages, of the Black woman who was
       largely responsible for the Montgomery, Alabama bus boycott
       which led to the rise in prominence of Martin Luther King,
       Jr. Written especially for young people and has several
       illustrations of Mrs. Parks. Discusses Rosa Park's life
       from her birth on February 4, 1913 to the end of the bus
       boycott in 1957. Mrs. Parks has been called "The Mother of
       the (Modern) Civil Rights Movement."

127   Gregory, Chester W. Women in Defense Work During World War
       II: An Analysis of the Labor Problems and Women's Rights.
       Jericho, New York: Exposition Press, 1974.
           There are various references to Black women in this book.
       There is one section in this work entitled "The Black Woman
       in War Work--1941-1945." The author discusses the many
       jobs Black women held during World War II: aircraft produc-
       tion, ordinance work, steel production, foundries, transpor-
       tation, and shipbuilding, etc.

128   Grier, William and Cobb, Price. Black Rage. New York: Basic
       Books, 1968.
           In one section two Black psychiatrists discuss the Black
       woman's identity crisis, which is brought on by her histori-
       cal relationship to the white community.

129   Grosnenor, Verta Mae. Thursdays and Every Other Sunday Off:
       A Domestic Rap. New York: Doubleday and Co., 1972.
           A collection of articles, quotations, stories, poems and
       letters by and about Black domestic servants. "Thursdays
       and every other Sunday will be your days off": with these
       words for years many of our mothers, grandmothers, sisters,
       aunts, uncles, cousins, and friends, and girlfriends entered
       domestic life.

130   Guadet, Frances Joseph. "He Leadeth Me." New Orleans: the
       Author, 1913.
           This short, 144 page autobiography is about a Black woman
       who was born in Mississippi in 1861 and later became founder
       of the Colored Industrial Home and School Association in New
       Orleans, and the President of the Woman's Christian Temper-
       ance Union of Louisiana. The author discusses what life was

(Guadet, Frances Joseph)
like for her and other Blacks in the United States during
the Reconstruction and Post-Reconstruction Period. Miss
Guadet also wrote about her travels to England and France.

131   Guffy, Ossie. Ossie: The Autobiography of a Black Woman.
      New York: W. W. Norton and Co., 1971.
      The story of a Black woman born and raised in Cincinnati
      during the depression. Examines the many things she had to
      contend with in raising her family, the welfare worker, pov-
      erty street gangs and a racist society. Tells of the dig-
      nity that Mrs. Guffy maintained through all her setbacks.

132   Hackley, Mrs. E. Azalia. The Colored Girl Beautiful. Kansas
      City, Mo.: Burton Publishing Co., 1916.
      Compiled from talks given to different schools at differ-
      ent times, this book is interesting for its historical per-
      spective. The racial advice is still sound today. It is
      very positive in approach, very loving and motherly in man-
      ner. It is valuable for showing what importance the Black
      race placed on physical and spiritual beauty more than 60
      years ago.

133   Hamilton, Kelly. Goals and Plans of Black Women: A Sociolog-
      ical Study. Hicksville, New York: Exposition Press, 1975.
      Compares the goals and aspirations of two groups of Black
      women--a sample group from a predominately Black college and
      another group from an ethnically mixed university. The
      author concludes that social class tends to affect the stu-
      dents' levels of achievement, orientation, and educational
      aspirations and plans more than the type of school attended.

134   Hammond, Lily. In the Vanguard of a Race. New York: Council
      of Women from Home Missions and Missionary Education Move-
      ment of the United States and Canada, 1922.
      Several Black women are included in this work: Mrs.
      Nannie H. Burroughs, Mrs. Janie Porter Barret, Mrs. Maggie
      L. Walker, and Mrs. Martha Drummer.

135   Hansberry, Lorraine. To be Young, Gifted, and Black. Engle-
      wood Cliffs, New Jersey: Prentice-Hall, 1969.
      An autobiographical work by the first Black woman to pre-
      sent a play on Broadway. In 1959, Miss Hansberry presented
      "A Raisin in the Sun." In the same year the playwright won
      the Drama Critics Circle Award for her play.

136   Harris, Middleton. The Black Book. New York: Random House,
      1974.
      Various references are made to Black women throughout this
      book. There is much historical material on Black men and
      women, as well as many illustrations, sketches, drawings,
      and photos of the Black women included in this work.

137 Harrison, Juanita. My Great, Wide, Beautiful World. New
York: Macmillan, 1936.
An autobiographical account of a Black woman who was born
in 1891 and traveled through more than twenty countries
between 1927 and 1935. She would go to one country and work
while she was there and save up enough money so she could
travel to another one. The writer kept a diary of her travels and this book was published about a year after she
returned to America.

138 Haviland, Laura S. A Woman's Life-Work: Labors and Experiences of Laura S. Haviland. Reprint of the 1887 edition
published by C. V. Waite and Co., Chicago. Miami, Florida:
Mnemsyne Publishing Co., Inc., 1969.
This white missionary and abolitionist makes references to
a number of Black women. Of particular interest is a Black
woman slave, Milla Granson, who taught other slaves how to
read and write, and a number of other Black female slaves
who worked for their freedom and that of their children by
doing extra jobs. There are also references to other Black
female slaves that the author helped to acquire their freedom. Several Black women are included in this collection:
Harriet Tubman, Phillis Wheatley, and Sojourner Truth.

139 Hedgeman, Anna Arnold. The Trumpet Sound: A Memoir of Negro
Leadership. New York: Holt, Rinehart and Winston, 1964.
An autobiography of a Black woman who grew up in a small
Midwestern town during the early 1900s and became a teacher
in the South. Because of her unpleasant experiences in the
South she returned to the North and organized people to help
eliminate the cruelty of the southern part of the country.
She worked with a number of Black leaders over the years to
help gain human dignity for Black people.

140 Heilbrut, Tony. The Gospel Sound: Good News and Times. New
York: Simon and Schuster, 1971.
The author includes many Black women gospel singers and
groups in this work: Sallie Martin, Mahalia Jackson, Bessie
Griffin, Roberta Martin, Dorothy Love Coates, Rosetta
Tharpe, Marion Williams, Shirley Caesar, Deloris Barrett
Campbell, Willie Mae Ford Smith, Clara Ward, Ruth Davis, The
Staple Singers, The Caravans, The Davis Sisters, and The
Ford Sisters. Many of the above discuss the forces that
inspired them and the influence that gospel music has had on
their lives. There are also several photos included in this
book as well as a discography of each person or group.

141 Helm, Mary. From Darkness to Light: The Story of Negro Prog-
ress. Reprint of the 1909 edition published by Fleming
Revell Co., New York. Westport, Conn.: Negro Universities
Press, 1969.

(Helm, Mary)
There is one section in this work on "Work of the Woman's Home Missionary Societies." The lack of an index seriously hampers this effort because individuals are not easily identified. Whole sections must be read to gather information concerning women.

142 Hernton, Calvin C. Sex and Racism in America. Garden City, New York: Doubleday, 1965.
Includes a discussion on "The Negro Woman." Feels that the sexual atrocities the Black woman has suffered in the United States and the effect these atrocities have had on her personality is more bloody and brutal than most people can imagine.

143 _____. Coming Together: Black Power, White Hatred, and Sexual Hang-Ups. New York: Random House, 1971.
There are various references to the Black woman and sex throughout the books. Two chapters relate directly to the Black woman: "Historical Analysis of Black Sexuality in American Society," and "Social Psychiatry of Sexual Crisis Among Black Men and Women."

144 Hicks, Estelle Bell. The Golden Apples: Memoirs of a Retired Teacher. New York: Exposition Press, 1958.
A retired teacher writes about her experiences as an educator.

145 Higgins, Chester J. with text by Harold McDougall. Black Women. New York: The McCall Publishing Co., 1970.
A collection of photographs of Black women with brief opinions by Black women. The author praises Black womanhood and the life styles of many women: the young Black-power advocates, the fine Black beauties, the Black bourgeoisie, the unbroken Black grandmothers, and those who just live from day to day.

146 Hill, Robert. Black Families: Their Strengths and Stability. New York: Emerson Hill Publishing Co., 1972.
The author points out the historic relationship of the Black woman in the family structure in the Black community. He disagrees with many of the past assumptions by E. Franklin Frazier (See 114, 115).

147 Holcombe, Return I. A Biography of Carver and Hennepin Counties, Minnesota. New York: H. Taylor and Co., 1972.
An account of a case in which a Black slave woman was freed at a trial held in Hennepin County. Also records the courtroom scene at the trial.

148 Holdredge, Helen (O'Donnell). Mammy Pleasant. New York: Putnam, 1953.

(Holdredge, Helen)
The biography of a Black woman who was born a slave in Georgia and later made her way to San Francisco to become the owner of the most fashionable boarding houses in the city. Mrs. Mary Ellen Pleasant assisted many of the fugitive slaves who came to her in San Francisco from the agents of the Underground Railroad before the Civil War. Mrs. Pleasant died in 1904. Several photographs of Mrs. Pleasant included.

149   Holiday, Billie. Lady Sings the Blues. Garden City, New York: Doubleday, 1956.
The autobiography of the famous blues singer. Miss Holiday tells of her experiences as a Black woman, child, rise to fame, and her fight with drugs. The reader gains many insights into the private life of a complex Black woman.

150   Holt, Hamilton. The Life Stories of Undistinguished Americans as Told by Themselves. New York: James Potts and Co., 1906.
Many of the stories in this collection include those of Black women. Some were ex-slaves and tell of their memories of slavery.

151   Holt, Rackham. Mary McLeod Bethune: A Biography. New York: Doubleday, 1964.
A biography of the great educator and advisor to Presidents. Discusses her early childhood in South Carolina and and the people she loved and respected. Great detail is given to Mrs. Bethune's philosophy on womanhood and race relations.

152   Horne, Lena. Lena. Garden City, New York: Doubleday, 1965.
The autobiography of the famous actress and singer. She tells of her early childhood and later life. A good deal of the book deals with her life at the Cotton Club in New York to her acclamation on television.

153   Horne, Lena and Moss, Carlton. In Person Lena Horne. New York: Greenberg Publisher, 1950.
A semi-autobiographical work about a Black woman who became a famous actress. Miss Horne writes of her struggle for stardom.

154   Houston, Ruby R. I was Afraid to be Happy. New York: Carlton Press, 1967.
The author gives a straightforward account of her life and the many complex problems she encountered in romances, marriages, jobs, and poverty in this short forty-eight page book. Tells of her life in Memphis, Tennessee and later in Chicago, Illinois.

155   Huie, William Bradford. <u>Ruby McCollum: Woman in the Suwanee</u>
      <u>Jail</u>. New York: New American Library, 1964.
        Written by a white journalist about Ruby McCollum who
      spent two years in Florida's Suwanee County Jail for killing
      a white doctor who fathered one of her children. She was
      convicted in 1952 and after serving her sentence, spent
      twenty years in a mental hospital in Chattahoochee, Florida.
      She was finally freed in 1974 and lives with her daughter in
      Ocala, Florida.

156   Hunter, Jane Edna Harris. <u>A Nickel and a Prayer</u>. Nashville,
      Tennessee: Parthenon Press, 1940.
        The autobiography of a Black woman who dedicated her life
      to the removal of some of the hazards facing young Black
      girls searching for decency and livelihood. Mrs. Hunter
      accomplishes her goal by establishing the Phillis Wheatley
      Association in 1911. She discusses her early childhood in
      South Carolina and the experiences in her life that led her
      to help other young Black working girls. Mrs. Hunter's
      religious upbringing and faith in God is seen throughout the
      book.

157   Hunton, Addie and Johnson, Kathryn M. <u>Two Colored Women with</u>
      <u>the American Expeditionary Forces</u>. Brooklyn, New York:
      Eagle Press, 1920.
        The personal narratives of two Black women who served and
      worked with the United States Army in Europe between 1914–
      1918. They discuss their war work and their relationships
      with the Y.M.C.A., and other welfare organizations. Their
      work was limited to Black soldiers only. The writers also
      discuss how Black soldiers were discriminated against and
      how they helped to change all that.

158   Hurston, Zola Neale. <u>Dust Tracks on a Road: An Autobiog-</u>
      <u>raphy</u>. Philadelphia: J. B. Lippincott, 1942.
        An autobiography of a Black woman from Florida who became
      an outstanding and respected anthropologist and novelist.
      Describes the long and sometimes dusty road that she trav-
      eled to accomplish her goals. This work is more than a
      story of her life, it is filled with her reflections on
      Black religion and culture and her philosophy of life.

159   Jackson, Jesse. <u>Make a Joyful Noise Unto the Lord: The Life</u>
      <u>of Mahalia Jackson, Queen of Gospel</u>. New York: Thomas
      V. Crowell Co., 1974.
        One of the latest biographies on Mahalia Jackson, "Queen
      of Gospel." Much of the material in this book has appeared
      elsewhere and it gives the reader very little new insight in
      the life and times of Miss Jackson. It is written in
      straightforward language.

160   Jackson, Jacquelin Johnson. "Black Female Sociologists." In
      Black Sociologists: Historical and Contemporary Perspec-
      tives. Edited by James E. Blackwell and Morris Janowitz.
      Chicago; University of Chicago Press, 1974.
         A study of Black sociologists compared by sex. Concludes
      that greater development and utilization of Black female
      sociologists could well be a major factor in improving sig-
      nificantly our knowledge and understanding of Blacks and of
      Black-White relationships in the United States. A partial
      bibliography in included.

161   ____. "Black Women in a Racist Society." In Racism and Men-
      tal Health. Edited by Charles V. Willie, Bernard M. Kramer,
      and Bertram S. Brown. Pittsburgh: University of Pitts-
      burgh Press, 1973.
         Reflects on the Black matriarchal and emasculatory theo-
      ries, with the conclusion that they serve as masks for white
      racism and imply the subjugation of the Black woman as a
      sine qua non for Black racial progress. The myths of the
      presumed superiority of Black women, particularly in rela-
      tionship to Black men are destroyed by an analysis of demo-
      graphic data relative to education, occupation, employment,
      income, and family stability. Suggests the importance of
      the Black sex ratio in any evaluations of Black family life
      and stresses the imperative of simultaneous priorities for
      both racial and sexual liberation for Black women now.

162   Jackson, Mahalia and Whylie, Evan McLeod. Movin' On Up.
      New York: Hawthorne Books, 1966.
         An autobiography of "The world's greatest gospel singer."
      Miss Jackson writes of her early life in New Orleans and
      Chicago where she migrated as a teenager. Gives the reader
      a glimpse into her inner faith of God and mankind. She also
      tells of the discrimination that she encountered while she
      was touring the country because she was Black.

163   Jacobs, Harriet Brent. Incidents in the Life of a Slave Girl,
      Written by Herself. Edited by L. M. Child. Boston, 1861.
         Tells about the institution of slavery and how it affected
      her life. She sees it as one of the most barbarous systems
      to ever develop in America. One of the earliest narratives
      by a former slave.

164   Jenness, Mary. Twelve Negro Americans. New York: Friendship
      Press, 1936.
         Included are several Black women: Lillian S. Procter,
      social worker; Mary E. Branch, President of Tillotson Col-
      lege; Juanita Jackson, Vice-President of the Methodist Youth
      Council in Evanston, Illinois in 1934; Esther Brown, field
      worker for the Women's Auxiliary of the Episcopal Church;
      and Juliette Derricotte, Trustee of Talladega and worker
      with Y.W.C.A.

165   Johnson, Clifton H., Editor. God Struck Me Dead: Religious
       Conversion Experiences and Autobiographies of Ex-Slaves.
       Philadelphia: Pilgrim Press, 1959.
           A number of Black ex-slave women are included in this
       collection. They reveal how God struck them and how they
       experienced a religious conversion. The value of these
       narratives does not lie in their factual content or the
       accuracy of detail of the reminiscences, but in the tone
       or general mood they convey.

166   Johnson, Georgia Douglas. The Heart of a Woman and Other
       Poems. Reprint of the 1918 edition published by the author.
       Freeport, New York: Books for Libraries Press, 1972.
           One of a number of early books of poetry written by a
       Black woman. In it she reveals that reality of a woman's
       heart and experience with astonishing ecstasy. In these
       poems one sees the secrets of a Black woman's nature, a
       privilege all the better understood when given with such
       exquisite utterance and with such a lyric sensibility.

167   Jones, Lois Mailou. Reflective Moments. Boston: The Museum
       of the National Center of Afro-American Artists, 1973.
           A short biographical sketch of Lois Mailou Jones, one of
       the most outstanding Black female artists in America. The
       artist was born in Boston, in 1905 and her exhibits have
       appeared in Europe as well as the United States. Miss Jones
       has been a beacon of inspiration to generations of Black
       artists.

168   Jordan, June. Fannie Lou Hamer. New York: Thomas Y. Crowell
       Co., 1972.
           A short (41 pages) biography about Fannie Lou Hamer, a
       Black woman born of poor parents in Mississippi on October
       6, 1917, who rose to become a leader of poor people. Mrs.
       Hamer organized voter registration drives in Mississippi and
       throughout the South. In 1964 she helped form a new Missis-
       sippi Democratic Party, a party that would let everyone
       vote. She also formed a Freedom Farm Cooperative, which
       encompasses 640 acres and serves more and more poor people
       who live near enough to know about it. Written for young
       people and includes several illustrations.

169   _____. Some Changes. New York: E. P. Dutton & Co., Inc.,
       1971.
           A collection of poetry by a Black woman poet. This short,
       eighty-five page book of poetry covers a variety of topics.
       Miss Jordan wants the listener to feel what she feels, see
       what she sees, and then do with it what he may. Hopefully,
       he (or she) will become more human, more caring, more
       intensely alive to the suffering and the joy.

170   Josey, E. J. What Black Librarians are Saying. Metuchen,
      N. J.: Scarecrow Press, 1972.
         A collection of articles by many Black women and men
      librarians. Even though most of the articles are by Black
      women, conspicuously absent are writings by the three best
      known Black librarians in the United States: Dorothy
      B. Porter, Jessie Carney Smith, and Ann Allen Shockley.

171   Keckley, Elizabeth. Behind the Scenes: or Thirty Years a
      Slave and Four Years in the White House. Buffalo, New York:
      Stansil and Lee, 1931.
         An autobiography of a Black woman who was a slave from
      Virginia and later purchased her son's freedom and her own
      while earning a living as a dressmaker. As a confidential
      friend and employee of Abraham and Mary Todd Lincoln, Mrs.
      Keckley spent a large part of her time in the White House.
      A number of personal letters from Mrs. Lincoln to Mrs.
      Keckley are included.

172   King, Coretta. My Life with Martin Luther King, Jr. New
      York: Holt, Rinehart and Winston, 1969.
         The autobiography of the widow of the slain Civil Rights
      leader Martin Luther King, Jr. Gives a personal view of her
      family and the background to get a better understanding of a
      great man. She also gives a challenge to fulfill her hus-
      band's dream of human dignity for all mankind.

173   Kitt, Eartha. Thursday's Child. New York: Duell, Sloan and
      Pearce, Inc., 1956.
         The autobiography of the famous singer, dancer, and
      actress. Miss Kitt writes about how she grew up in the
      South and later moved to New York and became an actress.

174   Kletzing, H. F. and Crogman, W. H. Progress of a Race or the
      Remarkable Advancement of the Afro-American. Atlanta:
      J. L. Nichols and Co., 1897.
         Discusses "The Colored Woman of Today," and attempts to
      show that "above all let the Negro know that the elevation
      of his race can come only, and will come surely through the
      elevation of its women." A number of photos of Black women
      are also included.

175   Kyte, Elizabeth L. Willie Mae. New York: Knopf, 1959.
         A novel about a southern Black woman, Willie Mae Cart-
      wright, based on a real person. The book centers around
      Willie Mae and her relationship with Blacks and whites in
      the South and the way she perceived both groups. In a large
      sense it is an odyssey of almost any Southern Black.

176   Ladner, Joyce A. Tomorrow's Tomorrow: The Black Woman. New
      York: Doubleday, 1971.

(Ladner, Joyce A.)
  Gives the historical role of the Black woman in American
society and shows that she has been the carrier of Black
culture. The work is more socio-historical than historical
and psycho-social than social. It also forecasts the future
role of Black women in America.

177   Larsen, Nella. Passing. New York: Knopf, 1929.
  A novel about Clare, a Black woman, who passes for white
and thought she would find happiness in life. Later she
found that she could not be happy in that situation.

178   Lee, Jarena. Religious Experience and Journal of Mrs. Jarena
  Lee Giving an Account of her Call to Preach the Gospel.
  Philadelphia, 1849.
    A brief account of the religious life and times of Mrs.
  Lee. Reprinted in 1936.

179   Lee, Reba (pseud.). I Passed for White. New York: Longmans,
  Green, 1955.
    The story about a Black woman who passed for white. The
  author tells what it means to be on both sides of the color
  line.

180   Lerner, Gerda. Black Women in White America: A Documentary-
  History. New York: Pantheon, 1972.
    A collection of documents and writings by Black women on
  a variety of topics from Slavery to the present. Perhaps
  the best compilation of documents by Black women to date.
  Includes comprehensive bibliographical notes as well as a
  list of autobiographies and biographies of Black women.
  Edited by a white woman.

181   Locke, Alain. The Negro in Art. Reprint of the 1940 edition.
  Chicago: Afro-Am Press, 1969.
    Several Black women and their works are included in this
  pictorial record of Black arts and crafts: Mary Edmonia
  Lewis, Anne Walker, Meta Warrick Fuller, Lois Mailou Jones,
  and Laura Wheeler Waring. There is a short biographical
  sketch of each woman and many pictures of Black women, a
  number of which were done by Black women artists.

182   _____. The New Negro: An Interpretation. New York: Albert
  and Charles Boni, 1925.
    A collection of various topics by Blacks, and includes a
  discussion on Black women: "The task of Negro Womanhood."

183   Longsworth, Polly. Charlotte Forten, Black and Free. New
  York: Thomas Y. Crowell, 1970.
    A biography for young people on one of the most outstand-
  ing Black women in America. Much of the information on
  Miss Forten can be found in other works. Emphasizes her

(Longsworth, Polly)
later life and the influence that other Black leaders had on her. It also focuses on the environment around Miss Forten which helped to influence her thinking.

184 MacBrady, John E., Editor. A New Negro for a New Century. Chicago: American Publishing House, 1900.
Included in this collection are two chapters on the Black woman written by Fannie Barrier Williams: "The Club Movement Among Colored Women in America," and "The Clubs and Their Location in All the States of the National Association of Colored Women and Their Mission." There are several photos of women including Mrs. Booker T. Washington, Mrs. Mary L. Davenport, Miss Mattie B. Davis, etc. Short biographical sketches of Phillis Wheatley and Sojourner Truth are included.

185 Majors, Monroe Alphus. Noted Negro Women: Their Triumphs and Activities. Reprint of the 1893 edition. Freeport, New York: Books For Libraries Press, 1971.
More than 300 short biographical sketches are included. Many of the women were wives of outstanding Black men. There are several articles, letters, and poems by Black women and more than 60 photos and sketches of the women.

186 Martin, Fletcher. Our Great Americans: The Negro Contribution to American Progress. Chicago: Gamma Corporation, 1953.
Several short biographical sketches of Black women, including: Marian Anderson, Dorothy Maynor, Bessie Smith, Lena Horne, Ethel Waters, Sarah Vaughan, Katherine Dunham, Mahalia Jackson, Edith Sampson, Mary McLeod Bethune, and Zora Neale Hurston. Photos of each woman are also included.

187 Mason, Julian D., Jr. Editor. The Poems of Phillis Wheatley. Chapel Hill, N. C.: University of North Carolina Press, 1966.
The majority of the book is a collection of poems by Miss Wheatley, with a short biographical sketch of her at the beginning.

188 Massey, Mary Elizabeth. Bonnet Brigades. New York: Alfred A. Knopf, 1966.
The white author includes a discussion on the role Black women played in the American Civil War. They assisted whites in philanthropic endeavors, organized their own aid societies, took an active interest in Black soldiers and contrabands, volunteered their services in hospitals, and worked in battle areas.

189 McGovern, Ann. Runaway Slave: The Story of Harriet Tubman. New York: Four Winds Press, 1965.

(McGovern, Ann)
A biography of Miss Tubman written especially for young
people. The central theme of the book is that even though
Harriet Tubman "ran away" to freedom, she did not forget
about other Blacks that were still in slavery. Tells how
she helped other slaves to become free.

190   McNair, Barbara and Lewis, Stephen. The Complete Book of
Beauty for the Black Woman. Englewood Cliffs, New Jersey:
Prentice-Hall, Inc., 1972.
Miss McNair gives her personal beauty routine and warns
that it may not work for other women. The author believes,
first and foremost, that Black women should be aware of
themselves as individuals. No book, no expert, and no cos-
metic can give you a look--each individual has her own to
start with. Beauty comes from a combination of home structure, hair, features, and personality. Several photos of
the author illustrating how to apply beauty treatments.

191   Meltzer, Milton. In Their Own Words: A History of the American Negro 1865-1916. New York: Crowell, 1965.
A collection of letters, diaries, speeches, autobiographies, newspaper articles, and pamphlets written by Black
men and women.

192   Meriwether, Louise. Daddy was a Number Runner. Englewood
Cliffs, N. J.: Prentice-Hall, 1970.
An autobiographical novel about a twelve-year-old Black
girl and her family living in Harlem. Based on real life
experiences of Black peoples' hunger and pride, of despair,
courage, and lovingkindness. It is the story of a Black
child's growing sense of being one of the victims of a cor-
rupt society.

193   Metcalf, George R. Black Profiles. New York: McGraw-Hill,
1968.
A record of eleven Black men and women who strove to wash
away all traces of inequality in America. The two Black
women included in this book are Harriet Tubman and Rosa
Parks.

194   Milwaukee County Welfare Rights Organization. Welfare Mothers
Speak Out: We Ain't Gonna Shuffle Anymore. New York:
W. W. Norton and Co., 1972.
The welfare mothers of America, who are mostly Black, tell
what poverty is really like: How it feels to be subjected
to the indignities and dehumanization of the welfare system.
Most mothers see the "Family Assistance Plan," not as a
reform program but a step backward. The title of the book,
"We Ain't Gonna Shuffle Anymore" comes from the Welfare
Rights song.

195 Mitchell, George. I'm Somebody Important: Young Black Voices
     from Rural Georgia. Urbana, Ill.: University of Illinois
     Press, 1973.
        Of the six discussed in this book, three are Black young
     women: Betty Brown, Janice Rilely and Rosie Mae Davis.
     Each individual talked about her life and the life of Black
     people in the South and America. Most of the women gave the
     reader a better understanding of young Blacks in the rural
     South, because they talked about everything from their boy-
     friends to their solutions to today's racial problems.
     There are also several photos of these young people and
     their families in this book.

196 Mix, Sarah A. In Memory of Departed Worth: The Life of Mrs.
     Edward (Sarah A.) Mix, Written by Herself in 1880. Torring-
     ton, Conn.: Press of Register Printing Co., 1884.
        A short, twenty-four page, autobiography of the author and
     her account of her religious beliefs while living in New
     York and Connecticut.

197 Montgomery, Janey Weinhold. A Comparative Analysis of the
     Rhetoric of Two Negro Women Orators: Sojourner Truth and
     Frances E. Walker Harper. Hays: Fort Hays Kansas State
     College, 1968.
        The white author analyzes the rhetoric of both women and
     makes certain conclusions: Miss Truth's techniques were the
     logical outgrowth of her own experiences and knowledge of
     the Bible; Mrs. Harper was given the opportunity for educa-
     tion and experience in writing. Therefore, with experience
     in writing, many of her techniques were used for their
     effect. The writer shows how both Black women developed
     effective techniques of rhetoric which were largely influ-
     enced by their diverse backgrounds.

198 Moody, Ann. Coming of Age in Mississippi. New York: Dial
     Press, 1968.
        An autobiography of a young Black woman from Mississippi.
     Miss Moody writes of her childhood in the South, her high
     school and college days and her involvement in the Civil
     Rights Movement. One of a few books written by a young
     woman who tells what life was like for her during the early
     1960's when the Civil Rights Movement was affecting Blacks
     everywhere and especially in Mississippi.

199 Moore, Carman. Somebody's Angel Child: The Story of Bessie
     Smith. New York: Thomas Y. Crowell Co., 1969.
        A biography of the great Black blues singer who was called
     "Empress of the Blues." The author writes of her life in
     Chattanooga, Tennessee, from the 1900's to her death in
     1937. Miss Smith is captured in all her moods from her high
     spirits to her bleak despairs. A number of rare photos of
     Miss Smith are included, as well as a number of her songs.

200 Moore, Martha Edith Bannister. <u>Unmasked: The Story of My</u>
<u>Life on Both Sides of the Race Barrier</u>. New York: Exposi-
tion Press, 1964.
The autobiography of a Black woman who was Caucasian in
appearance and for twenty-five working years "passed" for
white. More than an autobiography, it is a story about people of a minority group in a provincial Northern city. She
shows how she has been discriminated against because she was
a woman, Black, and because of her political affiliation.
Mrs. Moore believes however, that her contribution to society, church, and friends have not been in vain.

201 Moore, William, Jr. and Wagstaff, Lonnie H. <u>Black Educators</u>
<u>in White Colleges</u>. San Francisco: Jossey-Bass Publishers,
1974.
Contends in a discussion on the Black woman in higher education, that much of what we know about Black women in
higher education has come from their autobiographies, letters, and papers. Black women's participation in higher
education was primarily through teaching and administration
in all-Black colleges.

202 Morton, Lena Beatrice. <u>My First Sixty Years: Passion and</u>
<u>Wisdom</u>. New York: Philosophical Library, 1965.
The autobiography of a Black woman in Kentucky during the
early 1900's, who later became the first Black to receive
a Ph.D. in English from Western Reserve University in 1947.
In this story, Dr. Morton continues her analysis of education. She is concerned that so many people fail to develop
their potentialities. She gives a ten-point plan for young
Blacks to develop self-respect and respect for others.

203 Mossell, N. F. <u>The Work of the Afro-American Woman</u>. Reprint
of the 1894 edition. Freeport, New York: Books For Libraries Press, 1971.
Discusses the achievements of Black women in a variety of
fields including literature, verse, and journalism. Includes
several poems by the author.

204 Mott, Abigail F., Compiler. <u>Narratives of Colored Americans</u>.
New York: William Wood and Co., 1875.
These narratives are valuable from a historic viewpoint.
Nothing new is added as far as Phillis Wheatley or Sojourner
Truth is concerned. But entries such as "Old Dinah," "Old
Susan," "The Wife," "Poor Sarah," "The Faithful Nurse,"
"Belinda Lewis," "Hospitable Negro Women," "Faith of a Poor
Blind Woman," and "Clarinda, a Pious Colored Woman," give
rise to new insight to the depth of oppression in this
country.

205 Moynihan, Daniel. <u>The Negro Family: The Case For National</u>
<u>Action</u>. Washington, D.C.: Government Printing Office,
March, 1965.

(Moynihan, Daniel)
Emphasizes the role of the woman in the Black family.
Concludes that the Black family is unstable, therefore when
Black families break up, the woman must assume the task of
being the breadwinner.

206   Muhammad, Elijah. Message to the Black in America. Chicago:
Muhammad Mosque of Islam #2, 1965.
Various references are made to Black women. Mr. Muhammad
sees women as property and he states that the first step is
the control and protection of women in order to return to
the land with a thorough knowledge of our own selves. He
orders the men of the Nation of Islam to put the women under
guard, to keep them imprisoned in order to protect and control them. He concludes that to become good Muslims, Black
women must become chattel once again, with good and loving
masters. Feels that Black women must be respected and honored as women.

207   Murray, Joan. The News: An Autobiography. New York: McGraw
Hill, 1968.
An autobiography sketch of a Black female newswoman with
WCBS-TV. An inside view of what breaking into a news field
can really mean--with no punches pulled. Miss Murray gives
a number of tips on how to be a successful newsperson.
About half the book is devoted to photos of the author.

208   Murray, Pauli. Proud Shoes: The Story of an American Family.
New York: Harper and Row, 1956.
An autobiographical work by a Black woman about her
grandfather who started a school in the South for the freed
men. A great deal of the book is devoted to her family's
history as well as the time in which she lived.

209   Myrdal, Gunnar. An American Dilemma: The Negro Problem and
Modern Democracy. New York: Harper and Row, 1944.
Brief references of Black women in education, employment,
industries, leadership, professions, in the Army and Navy,
and examines the parallels between the status of Black women
and Black men.

210   Nadelson, Regina. Who is Angela Davis? The Biography of a
Revolutionary. New York: Peter H. Wyden, 1972.
A biography of the Black militant, Angela Davis, by a
white woman. Much of the material was supplied by Miss
Davis and her parents. It discusses her life from childhood
in the South through her trial in 1972 in which she was
acquitted by a jury of all charges brought against her.
Much of this biography is subjective and superficial.

211   Newman, Shirlee P. <u>Marian Anderson: Lady from Philadelphia</u>.
      New York: Westminster Press, 1965.
         A biography of the famous internationally known Black
      singer. Gives a few new insights in the life and times of
      Miss Anderson, especially during her early life.

212   Noble, Jeanne L. <u>The Negro Woman's College Education</u>. New
      York: Bureau of Publications, Teachers College of Columbia
      University, 1956.
         An account of the historical development of collegiate
      education for Black women. Discusses the roles that society
      has permitted Black women to play and how these positions
      have influenced their higher education. Dr. Noble also dis-
      cusses the important issues in the education of Black women.
      There is information about the lives and opinions of more
      than 400 Black women who have 4 years or more of college
      education.

213   Northup, Solomon. <u>Twelve Years a Slave</u>. Edited by Sue Eakin
      and Joseph Logsdon. Reprint of the 1853 edition published
      by Northup. Baton Rouge: University Press, 1968.
         Even though this is a narrative of a free Black who was
      kidnapped in 1841 and rescued in 1853, many Black women's
      voices are heard throughout the book. The author tells of
      the help he received from Blacks.

214   Oliver, Paul. <u>Bessie Smith</u>. New York: A. S. Barnes and Co.,
      1961.
         One of the earlier biographies on the great Black jazz
      singer Bessie Smith. Somewhat subjective, however, gives
      some insights into the personal life of Miss Smith.

215   Ovington, Mary White. <u>Half a Man: The Status of the Negro in
      New York</u>. New York: Longmans, Green and Co., 1911.
         A study by a white author of the Black worker in New York
      City, particularly in the different professions as well as
      in business. Includes a chapter on the Black woman as the
      breadwinner in the Black family.

216   _____. <u>The Walls Came Tumbling Down</u>. New York: Harcourt,
      Brace and World, 1947.
         This moving story of the NAACP is told by a white author.
      She writes about her associations with Black men and women
      over a fifty year period.

217   _____. <u>Portraits in Color</u>. New York: Viking Press, 1927.
         A collection of sketches of the lives of twenty interest-
      ing Black men and women. The women include: Maggie Lena
      Walker, Janie Porter Barrett, and Meta Vaux Warrick Fuller.

218   Patterson, Katheryn M. <u>No Time for Tears</u>. Chicago: Johnson
      Publishing Co., 1963.

(Patterson, Katheryn M.)
   Delbert Patterson Jr. is the subject of this sentimental
autobiography of a Black woman's struggle to cope with her
hydrocephalic child. Katheryn herself, a victim of epi-
lepsy, felt punished twice over for life having dealt her a
double burden.

219   Parker, J. A. Angela Davis: The Making of a Revolutionary.
      New Rochelle, N. Y.: Arlington House, 1973.
         The first half discusses the many Black men in America
      who paved the way for Black revolutionaries like Miss
      Davis. The second half is devoted to Miss Davis but lacks
      any new insights on her.

220   Parker, Marjorie H. Alpha Kappa Alpha Sorority: 1908-1958.
      n. p.: n.p., 1958.
         The history of a Black woman's sorority and its impact on
      Black womanhood. Also lists a number of outstanding Black
      women who are members of that organization.

221   Parks, Lillian Roger. My Thirty Years Backstairs at the White
      House. New York: Fleet Publishing Company, 1961.
         An autobiography about a Black woman who was a maid in the
      White House. She writes of her personal experiences with
      the "First Families" in the White House between 1919 and
      1960.

222   _____. It Was Fun Working at the White House. New York:
      Fleet Publishing Co., 1969.
         This is a smaller version of the previous book. Illus-
      trated and written especially for young people. A new
      chapter added recounting her experience as a dinner guest of
      Lyndon B. Johnson when he was President.

223   Pauli, Hertha Ernestine. Her Name Was Sojourner Truth. New
      York: Appleton-Century Crofts, 1962.
         A biography of the great revolutionist and reformer
      Sojourner Truth. Miss Truth's capacity to rise by her own
      unaided efforts and become one of the leading religious and
      women's suffrage reformer of her day.

224   Peare C. O. Mary McLeod Bethune. New York: Vanguard Press,
      1951.
         A biography of the great Black educator. Much of the
      information on Miss Bethune in this book can be found in
      other sources.

225   Petry, Ann. Harriet Tubman: Conductor of the Underground
      Railroad. New York: Thomas Y. Crowell, 1955.
         A biography written for young people of the great aboli-
      tionist, Harriet Tubman, and her role in the underground
      railroad movement.

226 Pickard, Kate E. R. The Kidnapped and the Ransomed Being the
     Personal Recollections of Peter Still and His Wife, "Vina,"
     After Forty Years of Slavery. New York: W. T. Hamilton,
     1856.
          The title explains this book. Also discusses the insti-
     tution of slavery throughout the South. Special attention
     is devoted to slavery in Alabama and Kentucky. An appendix
     is included as well as several illustrations.

227 Picquet, Louisa. Louisa Picquet, the Octroon: Or Inside
     Views of Southern Domestic Life. New York: The Author,
     1861
          The author, who was forced to become a concubine of her
     master, revealed the shameful tenets of slavery. She ana-
     lyzes the master-female slave relationship, as well as the
     tales of Black females in bondage.

228 Pitrone, Jean Maddern. Trailblazer: Negro Nurse in the
     American Red Cross. New York: Harcourt, 1969.
          A biography of Frances Reed Elliot who in 1916 became the
     first Black nurse officially enrolled in the American Red
     Cross. She was thirty-one when she completed her training,
     and for the rest of her long life she never ceased caring
     for and about people. Miss Elliot served in World Wars I
     and II, the influenza epidemic of 1918, and the Depression.
     Written by a white woman.

229 Pleasants, Mary Minta. Which One? and Other Ante Bellum
     Days. Published by the Author in 1910. Reprinted by Books
     for Libraries Press, Freeport, New York in 1972.
          The author discusses four different types of house ser-
     vants in this book. She attempts to give an enlighting pic-
     ture of what house servants, including Black "mammies" were
     like in the Ante Bellum Days. Several Black "mammies" dis-
     cussed are: "Mammy Patsy," "Aunt Cindy," and "Mammy Jane."
     Miss Pleasants gives isolated incidents of a few slaves and
     presents a picture as applying to all Blacks during slavery.
     In other words, she gives the traditional stereotype view of
     Blacks during that era.

230 Ploski, Harry A. and Brown, Roscoe C. Negro Almanac. New
     York: Bilwether Publishing Co., 1967.
          Includes a section on the Black woman, covering the
     following topics: "Historical Perspectives," "Matriarchy
     and Current Trends," "Outstanding Black Women," and a "List
     of Additional Prominent Negro Women."

231 Porter, James A. Modern Negro Art. Reprint of the 1943 edi-
     tion. New York: Arno Press and The New York Times, 1969.
          Several Black women and their works are included:
     Edmonia Lewis, Ella D. Spencer, Lottie Wilson Moss, Meta
     Vaux Warrick Fuller, Laura Wheeler Waring, Lois Marlou Jones,

(Porter, James A.)
Augusta Savage, Elizabeth Prophet, Alice Elizabeth Catlett, Selma Burke, and Hilda Wilkerson. Contains eighty-five half-tone plates and many of these pictures are by Black women.

232 Potter, Merle. 101 Best Stories of Minnesota. Minneapolis: Harrison and Smith, 1931.
Included in this collection is the story of a Black slave who was brought to the city by her master and gained her freedom through forceful and legal action started by abolitionists.

233 Prince, Nancy. A Narrative of Life and Travels of Nancy Prince. Boston: The Author, 1850.
The life and experiences of a free Black woman born in 1799 in Newburyport, Mass. Mrs. Prince writes of her many travels throughout the world including: Copenhagen, England, Russia, and Jamaica. The author was also a teacher and Missionary. The religious upbringing is seen throughout the book.

234 Quarles, Benjamin. Black Abolitionists. New York: Oxford University Press, 1969.
The author includes the role Black women played in the abolitionist movement. The author's notes on bibliographical literature is most exhaustive and comprehensive and offers many leads for those wanting to know more about Black women's role in the abolitionist movement.

235 Radford, Ruby L. Mary McLeod Bethune. New York: G. P. Putnam's Sons, 1973.
Another short biography, 61 pages, of the great Black educator. Written especially for young people and has several illustrations of Mrs. Bethune. Traces the biographee's life from her birth in a log cabin near Mayesville, South Carolina, on July 10, 1875 to her death in Daytona Beach, Florida on May 18, 1955. In Mrs. Bethune's will she wrote these words to Black people everywhere: "I leave you love. I leave you hope. I leave you dignity."

236 Ray, Emma P. (J. Smith). Twice Sold, Twice Ransomed: Autobiography of Mr. and Mrs. L. O. Ray. Chicago: Free Methodist Publishing House, 1926.
The two individuals tell of their experiences in the South and West. They later become social workers and missionary workers for the church in Seattle, Washington in the late nineteenth and early twentieth century.

237 Reid, Inez Smith. "Together" Black Women. New York: Emerson Hall Publishing Co., 1971.

(Reid, Inez Smith)
Prepared for the Black Women's Community Development Foundation. It is basically information on "militant" Black women and men all over the U.S. who were interviewed and gave their opinions on a variety of subjects. This work is also a study of the Black community.

238   Richardson, Benjamin. Great American Negroes. New York: Crowell, 1945.
Twenty-one biographical sketches of which three are women--Marian Anderson, Katherine Dunham, and Mary McLeod Bethune. Contains only the traditional group of celebrities. Pen and ink drawings of the biographees are included.

239   Richings, G. F. Evidences of Progress among Colored People. Philadelphia: Ferguson, 1909.
Includes a chapter on "Prominent Colored Women." Also mentions Black women in other fields of endeavor such as journalism, education, and religion. A number of photos of Black women are included.

240   Richmond, M. A. Bid the Vassal Soar: Interpretive Essays on the Life and Poetry of Phillis Wheatley and George Moses Horton. Washington, D. C.: Howard University Press, 1974.
Sixty-six pages are devoted to Mrs. Wheatley, as well as twelve pages of notes on her. The author discusses the poet in nine chapters: "The Poet and the General (Washington)," "From a Fancide Happy Seat," "A Child Prodigy," "Poetry and Flame," "Triumph in London," "War, Revolution, Freedom," "Marriage," "Tragedy and Death," and "The Critics." Some of the material on Phillis Wheatley has appeared elsewhere. The Notes at the end of the section on the poet are very detailed and will lead the reader to additional sources on the life and poetry of Phillis Wheatley.

241   Robeson, Eslands Cardoza Goode. African Journey. New York: John Day and Co., 1945.
An autobiographical work by the wife of a famous Black man, Paul Robeson. Written in a journalistic manner describing her daily impressions and conversation with the people of the motherland. Shows the importance of African liberation and the need for a Pan-African movement. This book was written at a time when there was only two independent African countries. There are also several illustrations in the book.

242   Robinson, Wilhelmina S. Historical Negro Biographies: International Library of Negro Life and History. New York: Publishers Co., 1967.
There are nearly fifty biographies on Black women in this work from various fields. Many sketches and photos are included of the women: Phillis Wheatley (1753-1784-Poetess),

(Robinson, Wilhelmina S.)
Carolina Virginia Anderson (1848-?-Physician), Ida B. Wells
Barnett (1862-1931-Civil Rights Worker), Fanny M. Jackson
Coppin (1836-1913), Mme. Bernard Couvent (?-1936-Philanthro-
pist), Ellen Craft (fugitive slave), Catherine Ferguson
(Pioneer in Welfare Work), Elizabeth Taylor Greenfield
(1809-?-Concert Singer), Charlotte L. Forten (1838-1915-
Abolitionist and Teacher), Frances Ellen Watkins Harper
(1825-1911), Edmonia Lewis (1845-?-Sculptress), "Mammy"
E. Pleasants/Mrs. Alexander Smith (?-1904-Financial Sup-
porter of John Brown), Fannie M. Richards (1840-1923-Teach-
er), Mary Burnett Talbert (1886-1923-Worker for Civil Rights
and the Red Cross), Sojourner Truth (1797-1883-Civil War
Heroine and Abolitionist), Harriet Tubman (1823-1913-Aboli-
tionist and Conductor of the Underground Railroad), Sarah
Breedlone "Madame" Walker (1869-1919-Cosmetic Manufacturer),
Maggie Lena Walker (1867-1934-Banker), Gertrude E. Fisher
Anderson (1894-?-Candy Manufacturer), Marian Anderson
(1908-?-Singer), Josephine Baker (1907-1975-Entertainer and
Humanitarian), Daisy Gaston Bates (1922-, Civil Rights Work-
er), Mary McLeod Bethune (1875-1955-Educator), Jane Matilda
Bolin (1908-, Judge), Gwendolyn Brooks (1917-, Poet),
Charlotte Brown Hawkins (1883-, Educator), Hallie Quinn
Brown (1849-1949-Teacher and Elocutionist), Katherine
Dunham (1910-, Dancer and Choreographer), Althea Gibson
(1927-, Athlete), Lena Horne (1917-, Singer and Actress),
Bernice Gaines Hughes (1904-, Officer in the U.S. Women's
Army Corps), Zora Neale Hurston (1903-1960-Anthropologist
and Novelist), May Howard Jackson (1912-, Sculptor),
Elizabeth Duncan Koontz (1919-, Educator), Hattie McDaniel
(1898-, Actress), Addie Mitchell (1884-1960-Singer),
Constance Baker Motley (1921-, Judge), Jeanne L. Noble
(1926-, Educator), Ann Lane Petry (1912-, Author), Mary
Leontyne Price (1927-, Opera Singer), Wilma Glodean Rudolph
(1940-, Athlete), Edith Spurlock Sampson (1901-, Delegate to
the United Nations), Augusta Savage (1900-, Sculptor),
Philippa Duke Schuyler (1932-, Musician), Mary Church
Terrell (1863-1954-Civic Leader), and Ethel Waters (1900-,
Actress).

243   Rollins, Charlemae Hill. They Showed the Way: Forty
      American Negro Leaders. New York: Thomas Y. Crowell Co.,
      1964.
         Of the forty Black American leaders discussed, eight are
      women: Ida Wells Barnett, Mary McLeod Bethune, Deborah
      Gannet, Frances Ellen Watkins Harper, Edmonia Lewis, Harriet
      Tubman, Maggie Lena Walker, and Phillis Wheatley. The book
      is indexed.

244   Rutland, Eva. The Trouble with Being a Mama. Nashville,
      Tennessee: Abingdon Press, 1964.

(Rutland, Eva)
   A Black mother's account of her life with four lively,
lovable and troublemaking youngsters. Tells of the dilemmas, the anxieties, and the joys of being the mother in a
family growing up in America in the late 1960's. Even
though being a mama is the same the world over. Mrs.
Ruthland shows how Black mothers have additional problems.

245   Sams, Jessie Bennett. White Mother. New York: McGraw-Hill,
      1957.
   The autobiography of two Black twin girls and the Southern
white woman who took them in. Discusses the love that was
shown between the two little Black girls and the white
mother in a small Florida town. Mentions the problems that
the white woman encountered as well as the racist tenets of
southern society.

246   Scanzoni, John H. The Black Family in Modern Society.
      Boston: Allyn and Bacon, 1971.
   A study of 400 male led Black families in Indianapolis.
Much attention is devoted to discussing Franklin Frazier's
supposition that economic betterment of Black families
would strengthen it.

247   Shackelford, Jane Dabney. My Happy Days. Washington, D.C.,
      The Associated Publishers, Inc., 1944
   Tells of the author's experiences with life and how she
coped with it. She discusses many of the social customs of
Black people and how many of them have been misunderstood.
Tells of the conditions of Black children. A number of pho-
tos are included.

248   Schultz, David A. Coming Up Black: Patterns of Ghetto So-
      cialization. Englewood Cliffs, N. J.: Prentice-Hall, 1969.
   An intensive study of a small number of project families.
Seeks to answer the questions of how poor migrant Black families make a life for themselves in the cities. There are
several studies on the role of the Black mother as she pre-
pares her children to live in the depriving and hostile
world in which they are born.

249   Schuyler, Philippa Duke. Adventures in Black and White. New
      York: Robert Speller and Sons, Publishers, 1960.
   This outstanding Black woman musical performer and com-
poser writes about the people, places, where she went, what
she saw, and what she learned in her travels all over the
world between 1954 and 1960. The writer traveled and per-
formed in Mexico, Cuba, London, Paris, Madrid, Turkey, and
Africa.

250   Scruggs, Lawson Andrew. Women of Distinction. Raleigh,
      N. C.: L. A. Scruggs, 1893

(Scruggs, Lawson Andrew)
A collection of short biographies of nearly one hundred outstanding Black women. Many of the biographies have appeared in other works. However, there are several chapters on the Black women: "Afro-American Women in the Home." Several photos of many women are also included.

251 Shepperd, Gladys Byram. Mary Church Terrell: Respectable Person. Baltimore: Human Relations Press, 1959.
The story of Mary Church Terrell and how she fought to gain respectability and prestige for Black people by breaking down the barriers of discrimination in the restaurants and eating places in the nation's capital. Mrs. Terrell was President of the Co-ordinating Committee for the Enforcement of the District of Columbia Anti-Discrimination Laws. The greatness of Mrs. Terrell's life lay in the way she met life and bent it to her purpose. This book also discusses Mrs. Terrell's childhood, her education at Oberlin College, her marriage, and her early career as a leader of her people and desire for equal justice for all under the law.

252 Sirkis, Nancy. One Family. Boston: Little, Brown and Co., 1970.
A biographical sketch of a Black welfare mother, in New York, Mrs. Frances Black, who had borne fourteen children, and yet refused to let the system crush her down. Mrs. Black makes her problems common ones that any head of a household must face at one time or another. There are more than seventy-five photos of Mrs. Black and her family in this one-hundred and twenty-five page book, written by a white woman.

253 Smith, Amanda. An Autobiography of Mrs. Amanda Smith: The Colored Evangelist. Chicago: Meyer and Brother, 1893.
Amanda Smith a Black Methodist Missionary who toured and preached the gospel not only in the United States but in parts of Western Europe, Africa and India, was a slave-born freewoman of remarkable mystical persuasion. She adopted two children in Africa. Took one to England for education and then returned to the U.S. in the 1890s. She died in Florida in 1915.

254 Staples, Robert. The Black Family: Essays and Studies. Belmont, California: Wadsworth Publishing Company, 1971.
About three-fourths of this book is devoted to the Black women. Some of the essays especially related to her include: "The Changing Role of the Black Woman to Black Man," "Unwed Mothers and their Sex Partners," and "The Black Prostitute in White America." Many of these essays have appeared in other publications.

255   Staples, Robert. <u>The Black Woman in America: Sex, Marriage, and the Family</u>. New York: Nelson-Hall Publishers, 1973.
       This book explores the psycho-social dimensions of the sexual, marital, and familiar roles Black women play and have played in American society. The central theme is that Black women have been oppressed as a result of their biological characteristics--their sex and race. It has an excellent bibliography.

256   Staupers, Mabel Keaton. <u>No Time for Prejudice: A Story of Integration in Nursing in the United States.</u> New York: Macmillan, 1961.
       Written against a background of the times and events that, since 1879, have affected the lives of all Blacks, including nurses. It tells the reasons it was necessary to establish schools for Black students who desired to become nurses. Also gives the motives that impelled the Black nurse pioneers to establish a special nursing organization, the National Association of Colored Graduate Nurses, in 1908. The author, a registered nurse, documented her book from the official records, correspondence and statements found in the files of the NACGN, as well as from personal interviews from both Black and white nurses.

257   Sterling, Dorothy. <u>Freedom Train: The Story of Harriet Tubman</u>. New York: Doubleday and Company, 1954.
       An early biography written for children and young people on the leader of the Underground Railroad and her leadership in it.

258   Sterne, Emma Gelders. <u>Mary McLeod Bethune</u>. New York: Knopf, 1957.
       The life and times of the great Black educator Mary McLeod Bethune. Much of the material is narrative in form and has been used in other sources. Written especially for young adults.

259   _____. <u>I Have a Dream</u>. New York: Knopf, 1965.
       Short biographies of three Black women who have been active in the Civil Rights Movement: Marian Anderson, Rosa Parks, and Daisy Bates.

260   Steven, Janet. <u>Marian Anderson: Singing to the World</u>. Chicago: Encyclopedia Britannica Press, 1963.
       A biography of one of the greatest singers America has ever known. Written in simplistic narrative form that traces her rise from her early years in international acclaim on the concert stage. Several photos are included.

261   Stewart, Maria W. <u>Meditations from the Pen of Mrs. Maria W. Stewart</u>. Washington: Enterprise Publishing Co., 1879.

(Stewart, Maria W.)
Most of the "meditations" are religious in nature, the author's philosophy on other subjects is included. Emphasizes special role that Black women owe to themselves and their people. Three addresses of the author are included: "An Address Delivered before the Africa-American Female Intelligence Society of Boston," "An Address Delivered at the African Masonic Hall, Boston, February 27, 1833," and "Mrs. Stewart's Farewell Address to her Friends in the City of Boston, Delivered September 21, 1833." Mrs. Stewart was perhaps the first American born Black woman to lecture publically.

262   Stewart-Baxter, Derrick. Ma Rainey and the Classic Blues Singer. New York: Stein and Day, 1970.
Short biographical sketches of several Black women blues singers: Mamie Smith, Lucille Hegamin, Edith Wilson, Rosa Henderson, Ma Rainey, Bessie Smith, Ida Cox, Victoria Spivey, Clara Smith, Sippie Wallace, Bertha "Chippie" Hill, Maggie Jones, Alberta Hunter, Faye Barnes, Martha Copeland, Lizzie Miles, Trixie Smith, Ada Brown, Cleo Gibson, Edmonia Henderson, Virginia Liston, Rosetta Howard, Lil Green, Viola Wells, and Jeanne Carroll. A survey of the classic Blue era and the contribution of the Black women singers to that period is included. There are photos of each singer as well as a discography of each singer's records.

263   Still, William. Underground Railroad. Philadelphia: Porter and Coates, 1872.
Includes the heroic deeds that Black women played in the Underground Railroad. Also discusses the conditions in America and how Black people were affected by them during the 1800s.

264   Stoddard, Anne. Top Flight: Famous American Women. New York: Thomas Nelson and Sons, 1946.
Marian Anderson is the only Black woman included in this collection of thirteen famous American women. Much of the biographical material on Miss Anderson has been printed elsewhere. The sketch on Miss Anderson is highly subjective and adds little knowledge to our understanding of her.

265   Stratton, Madeline R. Strides Forward: Afro-Afro-American Biographies. Lexington, Mass.: Ginn and Co., 1973.
Included are biographies of two Black women: Shirley Chisholm--stateswoman, and Sadie Alexander--lawyer. The author writes of Mrs. Chisholm's early childhood in Brooklyn, New York and the years of her later life and the training that prepared her for her election as the first Black Congresswoman. Sadie Tanner Mossell Alexander became the first Black woman in the United States to receive a Ph.D.

(Stratton, Madeline R.)
degree. She earned her law degree with high honors at the
University of Pennsylvania and became the first Black woman
admitted to the Pennsylvania Bar. Tells of Mrs. Alexander's
life from the day she was born on January 2, 1898 until the
present. There are several photos of both Mrs. Chisholm and
Mrs. Alexander.

266   Swift, Hildegard Hoyt. The Railroad to Freedom: A Story of
the Civil War. New York: Harcourt, Brace and Co., 1932.
The story of Harriet Tubman who escaped from her owners
and became a "conductor" on the Underground Railway. The
story is lively, spirited and adventurous. Mrs. Tubman died
in New York in 1913 following a very meaningful and match-
less life. Written for young readers.

267   Tarry, Ellen. The Third Door: The Autobiography of an
American Negro Woman. New York: David McKay, 1953.
The story of a Black woman born in the South, who was
denied a teaching position because she was a Catholic, moved
to New York, and became a writer of books for children and
articles. The title of her autobiography is derived from the
hope that there would be a third door free from social des-
ignations, that is, neither a door marked Black or White.

268   Taylor, Marshall W. The Life, Travels, Labors, and Helpers of
Mrs. Amanda Smith: The Famous Negro Missionary Evangelist.
Cincinnati: Cranston and Stone, 1887.
A fifty-nine page sketch of the life and labors of a Black
woman, Amanda Smith, who was born in 1836 in Maryland, and
later became an outstanding missionary in Africa and other
countries. Miss Smith is compared to other famous Black
women and men, and it is concluded that among the men of the
Black race and times, none equal Mrs. Smith as an instrument
of salvation for the human race.

269   Taylor, Susie King. Reminiscences of My Life in Camp with the
33rd United States Colored Troops. Boston: The Author,
1902.
Tells of the author's life with the Army and her early
childhood in Georgia where she learned how to read and
write. This is one of the few early autobiographies written
by a Black woman. Gives a good picture of what life was
like for Blacks during the 1800s.

270   Tcholakian, Arthur. The Majesty of the Black Woman. New
York: Van Nostrand Reinhold Co., 1971.
A photographic essay covering Black women from age eight
to ninety-nine. Most of the women are unknown. The essence
given is that the majesty of the Black woman is not only as
she is revealed in these extraordinary photographs but as

(Tcholakian, Arthur)
 she lives and breathes in her anonymous self, in this world
 and in this time.

271 Terrell, Mary Church. A Colored Woman in a White World.
 Washington, D.C.: Ransdell Publishing Company, 1940.
    The autobiography of a Black woman who was born in 1863
 in Tennessee and became a leading club woman and suffragist,
 lecturer, and writer. Miss Terrell graduated from Oberlin
 College in 1884 and later taught at Wilberforce University.
 She symbolizes the toil, the indomitable courage, the aspirations and tenacious determinations of Black people to move
 forward and upward. She earned respect and recognition in a
 "White World."

272 Thibodeaux, Sister Mary Roger. A Black Nun Looks at Black
 Power. New York: Sheed and Ward, 1972.
    A collection of poems on a variety of topics by a Black
 nun. The author finds herself in a dual role: being Black
 and a nun. There is one section of this book that deals
 with "Black Womanhood." Many photos of Black women, young
 and old, are included.

273 Thomas, Adam B. Pathfinders: A History of Progress of
 Colored Graduate Nurses. New York: Kay Printing House,
 1929.
    Discusses the problems that early Black nurses encounter
 while striving for recognition and acceptance as professionals. One of the earliest books on Black nurses. Later
 books usually cite material from this major work.

274 Thompson, Era Bell. American Daughter. Chicago: University
 of Chicago Press, 1946.
    The autobiography of a famous Black woman journalist. She
 tells about her childhood in Iowa and North Dakota, as well
 as her education in Iowa. The writer had many menial jobs
 until she worked for W. P. A. and desired to become a
 writer.

275 _____. Africa: Land of My Father. Garden City, New York:
 Doubleday and Co., 1954.
    A story of a Black American woman traveling in Africa and
 her experiences in several African countries. The author
 made her journey before most African countries gained their
 independence. She also discusses her own cultural shock
 while in the United States.

276 Thompson, Daniel C. Sociology of the Black Experience.
 Westport, Conn.: Greenwood Press, 1974.
    Deals mainly with the Black Ghetto and the Black family,
 with various references to the Black woman. The Black woman
 has been required to hold the Black family together, to set

(Thompson, Daniel C.)
goals, to stimulate, to encourage and protect both boys and girls.

277   Thompson, Mary Lou. <u>Forces of the New Feminism</u>. Boston: Beacon Press, 1970.

Deals mainly with the writings of White women. There are, however, several Black women: Elizabeth Duncan Koontz, "Women as a Minority Group"; Pauli Murray, "The Liberation of Black Women"; and Shirley Chisholm, "Women Must Rebel."

278   Tobias, Tobi. <u>Marian Anderson</u>. New York: Thomas Y. Crowell Co., 1972.

Another biography on the famous singer, Marian Anderson. This work has illustrations and was written especially for young adults. Very little new material is included.

279   Toppin, Edgar A. <u>A Biographical History of Blacks in America Since 1528</u>. New York: David McKay Co., 1971

Short biographies of twenty-two Black women, some contemporary, some older. Among them are: Mary Edmonia Lewis, first Black woman in America to be a sculptor (1845-1890); and Florence Mills, a leading Broadway star in the 1920s. Among the present day Black women included are: Janet Collins, the first outstanding Black in ballet; and Ella Fitzgerald, "The First Lady of Song."

280   Truth, Sojourner. <u>Narrative of Sojourner Truth</u>. Battle Creek, Michigan: the Author, 1878.

The life story of one of the most remarkable Black women ever. She was born a slave, gained her freedom and the freedom of her children and later became a staunch advocate of human dignity, women's rights, a nurse, and religious pathos. A number of Miss Truth's correspondence are also included.

281   Turner, Zatella Rowena. <u>My Wonderful Year</u>. Boston: Christopher Publishing House, 1939.

Description of the author's travels and experiences in England and Europe, and the things she saw and the people she met.

282   Turnor, Mae Caesar. <u>Memory Lane in My Southern World</u>. New York: Vantage Press, 1968.

The autobiography of a Black woman born in Texas in 1889. Miss Turnor's story concerns the twisted, tangled complexities that existed in the South during her childhood and how these experiences left a lasting impression on her. The author gives not only a history of her life, but also of the South.

283   Tyler, Ronnie C. and Murphy, Lawrence R. The Slave Narra-
       tives of Texas. Austin, Texas: The Encino Press, 1974.
         About half of these narratives are by Black women. This
       work is valuable because it explains the ex-slaves view-
       points. This collection of slave narratives is the only one
       that exists for Texas. There are several photos of Black
       women, including one of Mary Kincheon Edwards, age 127. An
       appendix and bibliography is included.

284   Uggams, Leslie and Fenton, Marie. The Leslie Uggams Beauty
       Book. Englewood Cliffs, N. J.: Prentice-Hall, 1966.
        Miss Uggams gives insights into the different techniques
       for retaining youthfulness. Also gives tips on how one may
       bring out her own outstanding physical beauty.

285   Vehanen, Kosti. Marian Anderson: A Portrait. New York:
       McGraw, 1941.
        An account of Miss Anderson's European and American tours
       in the 1930's and 1940's. Many of her personal impressions
       were written down in order that the public could better
       understand her as a woman. The author was Miss Anderson's
       voice coach for the ten-year period he is writing
       about.

286   Veney, Bethany. A Narrative of Bethany Veney: A Slave
       Woman. Worcester, Mass.: A. P. Bickenell Press, 1890.
        The autobiography of a Black woman who was born a slave in
       Virginia in 1815. After gaining her freedom she lived the
       rest of her life in Worcester, Massachusetts, returning to
       the South several times to see her former master. She
       points out that after the South had lost the war, her ex-
       master no longer viewed her in the same light as he once
       did. Mrs. Veney was a deeply religious woman and her reli-
       gious philosophy is seen throughout the book.

287   Vivian, Octavia B. Coretta: The Story of Mrs. Martin Luther
       King, Jr. Philadelphia: Fortress Press, 1970.
        The first biography of Mrs. King written by one of her
       friends. Mrs. Vivian focuses especially on Mrs. King's
       relationship with her husband's work. She discusses
       Coretta's childhood, education and courtship. More than a
       biography, this work is an assessment of a woman with a com-
       mitment that remains unwavering in spite of the assassina-
       tion of her husband. She is determined to carry his work,
       the Civil Rights Movement, to its ultimate end--a Human
       Rights Movement. There are also a number of photos of Mrs.
       King and her family.

288   Vroman, Mary Elizabeth. Shaped into Its Purpose: Delta Sigma
       Theta--The First Years. New York: Random House, 1965.

(Vroman, Mary Elizabeth)
The history of a Black woman's sorority and the role that some Black women played in getting it established. It also mentions some of its most illustrious Black women members.

289 Walker, Alice. In Love and Trouble: Stories of Black Women. New York: Harcourt, Brace and Jovanovich, 1967.
These are stories of Black American women--female, Afro-American people minus the rhetoric, minus the unbearably beautiful and the unbearably harsh masks Black women have worn even into the bed of the men who could not reach them, and whom they could not reach. Walker has a lot to say and a commanding way of saying it. The book is contemplative as well as introspective.

290 Waters, Ethel. His Eye is on the Sparrow: An Autobiography. Garden City, New York: Doubleday, 1951.
Miss Waters' autobiography gives an account not only of her life as an entertainer but also of the life of Black entertainers during the vaudeville era. The reader also gets a glimpse of Miss Waters' candor and unextinguishable sense of humor.

291 _____. To Me It's Wonderful. New York: Harper and Row, 1972.
Miss Waters writes of her life with the Billy Graham Crusade, as well as her early life in show business. She tells why she decided to give up acting and take up the banner for Jesus Christ. Gives a good insight of Miss Waters' faith in God and what Christianity has meant to her. There are many rare photos of Ethel Waters as well as a discography of her recordings.

292 Watkins, Mel. To Be a Black Woman: Portraits in Fact and Fiction. New York: W. M. Morrow and Company, 1971.
A collection of excerpts on and by Black women and men and six white men that include sociological studies, autobiographies, poetry, fiction and essays. The intention is to dispel some of the illusions and misconceptions concerning Black women through the various writings of the contributors.

293 Weld, Theodore D. American Slavery As It Is: Testimony of a Thousand Witnesses. New York: American Anti-Slavery Society, 1839.
A number of the stories in this work include some about Black women. Most of the testimonies about the women deal with the inhumane treatments that they received. Much of the information was given by white abolitionists.

294 Wells, Ida B. A Red Record: Tabulated Statistics and Alleged Causes of Lynching in the United States, 1892-1894. Chicago: Donahue and Henneberry, 1895.

(Wells, Ida B.)
One of the first statistical pamphlets in the United States on the lynching of Blacks and others since the Emancipation Proclamation. The author attempted to convince America to inaugurate an era of law and order. Miss Wells was one of the earlier Blacks to speak out against lynching.

295 West, Dorothy. The Living is Easy. Reprint of the 1948 edition published by Houghton Mifflin Co., Boston. New York: Arno Press and The New York Times, 1969.
A novel about Blacks living in New England at the turn of the century. Gives a good idea how some Blacks living in that section of the United States viewed themselves and others. Many living in that area felt superior to southern Blacks, and to many dark skinned Blacks. Many of the psychological, social, and material dimensions of Black life in New England are brought out.

296 Williams, Reverend Issac. Aunt Sally; or the Cross the Way of Freedom; The Narrative of the Slave-Life and Purchase of the Mother of Reverend Issac Williams, of Detroit, Michigan. Reprint of the 1858 edition published by the American Reform Tract and Book Society. Miami, Florida: Mnemosyne Publishing Company, Inc., 1969.
The cross refers to the religious cross and the writer contends it was the way of freedom. There are several portraits of "Aunt Sally," her son and his family, as well as several songs and poems in this work.

297 Williams, Maria P. My Work and Public Sentiment. Kansas City, Mo.: Burton, 1916.
An autobiographical account of the author's life as a teacher and active member of the Republican Party. There is also a collection of letters, speeches, and essays on a variety of topics.

298 Williams, Ora. American Black Women in the Arts and Social Sciences: A Bibliographic Survey. Metuchen, N. J.: The Scarecrow Press, Inc., 1973.
Contains over 1200 entries of works by Black American women in the arts and social sciences, including movies, tapes, and recordings based on works written by Black women. There are several photographs of Black women.

299 Williams, Rose Berthenia Clay. Black and White Orange. New York: Vantage Press, 1961.
Autobiographical story about a young Black girl called Orange in Tampa, Florida and her dreams of becoming an actress and entertainer. A frankly candid book discussing her adventures in Chicago, Boston, and the magic city, New York, as well as her careers as an actress, and tennis player.

300   Willie Charles V., Editor. The Family Life of the Black
    People. Columbus, Ohio: Charles B. Merrill, 1970.
       A collection of twenty-six articles on the poor and
middle-class Black family. Unlike some anthologies on the
Black family, most of the articles in this work were written within the past fourteen years. Some of the articles
treat subjects that are usually neglected.

301   Woodward, Helen. The Bold Women. New York: Farrar, Straus
and Young, 1953.
       This book deals mainly with white women. Part Three, how-
ever, "Woman Rampant: Self-expression of a Sex," gives
approximately 30 pages to Harriet Tubman and Sojourner
Truth in a subtitled section, "Aren't I A Woman."

302   Wormley, Stanton L. and Fenderson, Lewis H. Many Shades of
Black. New York: William Morrow and Co., 1969.
       A collection of personal narratives and commentaries of
forty-two prominent Black Americans. Five women are among
the writers: Patricia Robert Harris, Lena Horne, Margaret
Walker, Diahann Carroll, and Flaxie. A brief biography of
each author precedes her or his essay.

303   Wright, Charlotte Crogman. Beneath the Southern Cross: The
Story of an American Bishop's Wife in South Africa. New
York: Exposition Press, 1955.
       A story of a Black American bishop's wife in South Africa
and her experiences and impressions of both Black and white
people while there.

304   Yetman, Norman R. Voices from Slavery. New York: Holt,
Rinehart and Winston, 1970.
       A collection of interviews with ex-slaves. Many of those
interviewed were Black women. These narratives represent a
broad sample of the slave population and provide an invaluable reference source for testing historical and social
scientific generalizations. All of the persons interviewed,
including the women, give keen insights on slave life during
slavery. Most of the women discuss their role during slavery and the influence their mothers had on the family.

305   Yost, Edna. American Women of Nursing. Philadelphia: J. B.
Lippincott Co., 1947.
       Included is one Black woman: Estelle Massey Riddle. Mrs.
Riddle was born in 1903, received her B.S. degree in 1930
and M.A. degree in 1931, the first ever awarded a Black
nurse. Mrs. Riddle almost left her profession because of
lack of opportunity, and discrimination. She remained how-
ever, in order to create increasing opportunities for other
Black nurses. She also served for five successive years as
President of the National Association of Colored Graduate
Nurses.

ANNOTATED ARTICLES

306   Adams, John H. Jr.   "Rough Sketches: A Study of the Features
       of the New Negro Woman."   The Voice of the Negro,
       (August 1904), pp. 223-226.
           Feels that Black women of the 1900s, as they impress them-
       selves in the world, are a growing factor for the good and
       that their beauty, intelligence and character are a factor
       for better social recognition.   Seven sketches of Black
       women are included.

307   Aldous, Joan.   "Wives' Employment Status and Lower Class Men
       as Husband-Fathers: Support for the Moynihan Thesis."
       Journal of Marriage and the Family, 31 (August 1969),
       pp. 469-476.
           Data collected from a sample of employed working-class
       white and Black husband-fathers which shows that Blacks
       whose wives are employed outside the home and share the
       breadwinner role are less active in household task perfor-
       mance and decision-making than Blacks whose wives are not
       employed.   This relationship held when controls for family
       size, income and age of youngest child were made.   When the
       wife because of her husband's unemployment must take over
       the chief provider role, these findings suggest that he will
       be even less apt to fulfill his responsibilities as husband-
       father.   These results appear to stem from the slavery era
       and past and present job discrimination against the Black
       male.   It is supported by the finding that a wife's employ-
       ment status does not appear to have a negative effect on a
       white man's participation in the family household task per-
       formance and decision-making.

308   "Althea's (Gibson) Odyssey."   Life, (July 2, 1956).
           Gives a brief history of the life of Althea Gibson, the
       first Black admitted in the U.S. Lawn Tennis Association in
       1950.   Althea Gibson was born in Harlem and rose to fame by
       winning virtually all the major tennis tournaments in the
       world.

309   Andrews, Robert G., "Quasi-Adoption: A New Approach to the
      Permanent Placement of Negro Children." Child Welfare,
      47: 583-586.
         Discusses the problems encountered by placement agencies
      when they attempt to find families for an increasing number
      of Black dependent children. Quasi-adoption is articulated
      as a solution to the problems.

310   Anthony, Mary. "Dean of the School Marms." Negro Digest,
      (May 1951), pp. 31-32.
         Article about Mrs. Charlotte Stephens, who in 1869, became
      the first Black teacher in Little Rock, Arkansas. She was
      also the first Little Rock woman, either Black or white, who
      has had, as of 1951, a school named for her.

311   Aptheker, Herbert. "The Negro Woman." Masses and Mainstream,
      (February 1949), pp. 10-17.
         Concentrates on the highlight of the history of Black
      women from a marxist class-oriented approach. "The base of
      the Black slave woman's super-exploitation was her position
      as a slave worker."

312   Ashe, Christy. "Abortion or Genocide." Liberator, (August
      1970), pp. 4-9.
         Article relating to the cries of "genocide" by Black mili-
      tants through birth control. Black doctors, William Darity,
      C. J. Wellington, Douglas Stewart, M. Alfred Haynes, and
      Benjamin Moor, all express concern with the concept of geno-
      cide through birth control.

313   Avery, Paul. "Mildred Harrison's Viet Nam Ordeal." Ebony,
      (May 1967), pp. 88-96.
         Miss Harrison was a Black American jazz singer who was
      entertaining American troops in Viet Nam, and was imprisoned
      by Vietnamese on a "technicality." This technicality was
      that she failed to list two checks on simple exit declara-
      tion form required of all persons leaving Viet Nam.

314   Bailey, Pearl. "This Time It's Love." Ebony, (May 1953),
      pp. 123-126.
         Famous singer-actress, Pearl Bailey, tells the story of
      her marriage to white Louis Bellson.

315   Baker, Joseph V. "The Twig-Bender of Sedalia." The Brown
      American, (Fall-Winter 1944-1945), pp. 8-12.
         Tells of Charlotte Hawkins Brown, Head of Palmer Memorial
      Institute, a private finishing school for Black men and
      women. The school is located in Sedalia, North Carolina.

316   Baraka, Imaum Amiri. "Black Women." The Black World, (July
      1970).

(Baraka, Imaum Amiri)
The Black woman must work hand in hand with the Black man. Concludes that the Black woman must first be able to teach our children and contribute to the social development of the nation.

317   Beasley, Joseph D., Hunter, C. L. and Fischer, A. "Attitudes and Knowledge Relevant to Family Planning Among New Orleans' Negro Women." American Journal of Public Health, 56 (November 1966), pp. 1846-1855.
A study made in New Orleans in 1965 about the amount of knowledge concerning the biologic facts of conception that Black women possessed. They found that only 13 percent of a sample of ever-married, ever-pregnant Black women under age 45 possessed "essential knowledge" on the subject.

318   Bell, Robert. "The Lower-Class Negro Mothers' Aspirations for Their Children." Social Forces, 43, (May 1965), pp. 493-500.
The data given supports the hypothesis that it is possible to distinguish different subgroups along the Black lower class continuum. Given the importance of the Black mother in the lower class Negro family, her values and aspirations for her children's future. Significant differences were found in the responses of "low status" and "high status" lower class mothers to questions concerning their aspirations for their children.

319   Bennett, Lerone. "The Negro Woman." Ebony, (August 1960).
In an age when Blacks and whites, men and women, are confused about the meaning of femininity, Black women must prove that women are also women.

320   _____. "Pioneers in Protest: Sojourner Truth." Ebony, (October 1964), pp. 62-70.
Article about Miss Truth, who was strong in the Abolition Movement, as well as the feminist movement. Miss Truth was the "first" Black woman to become an antislavery lecturer.

321   Bentley, Gladys. "I am a Woman Again." Ebony, (August 1952), pp. 92-98.
Famous entertainer tells how she found happiness in love after medical treatment to correct her strange affliction.

322   Berry, R. M. F. "Southern Training School for Colored Women." Good Housekeeping, 53 (October 1911), pp. 562-63.
Gives a brief description of the "Black Mammy Memorial Institute" and how the school is training Black women for domestic service. The article gives the illusion of progress.

323   Bethune, Mary McLeod. "Clarifying Our Vision with the Facts." Journal of Negro History, 23 (January 1938), pp. 12-15.

(Bethune, Mary McLeod)
> Mrs. Bethune discusses the need and importance of knowing about Black History and Culture. She concludes that by knowing this history, our youth will gain confidence, self-reliance and courage.

324 ____. "I Work With Youth." The Brown American, 1 (October 1939), p. 11.
> Concludes that it is one of the joys of her work with youth to see young men and women prepare for the workaday world.

325 ____. "My Last Will and Testament." Ebony, (September 1963), pp. 150-56.
> As life drew to a close, American's First Black Lady prepared for Black people a legacy of love. This legacy is discussed in this Special Issue.

326 Bishop, S. H. "Industrial Conditions of Negro Women in New York." Southern Workman, 39 (September 1910) p. 525.
> In the form of a letter written by Dr. Wm. J. Schieffelin, Chairman of the Committee on Improving Industrial Conditions of Negroes in New York City, it points out the fact that Black women are virtually excluded from industrial work in the city.

327 "Black Women Prefer Black Men." San Francisco Chronicles, 3 (December 1970).
> Several Black college women were interviewed to get their viewpoints on dating white men and interracial marriages.

328 Blake, Emma L. "Zora Neale Hurston: Author and Folklorist." Negro History Bulletin, 29 (April 1966), pp. 149-151.
> Gives a brief biographical sketch of Mrs. Hurston's life. Mrs. Hurston died on February 3, 1950.

329 Blauvelt, Mary Taylor. "The Race Problem: As Discussed by Negro Women." American Journal of Sociology, 6 (March 1901), pp. 662-72.
> An analysis of the race problem by members of the Michigan State Federation of Colored Women's Club. Issues focused on were the securing of a higher moral tone for the race and the development of skills. Emphasis was also placed on the development of self-respect, pride and the "Development of a pride in American-African manhood."

330 Bock, W. Wilbur. "Farmer's Daughter Effect: The Case of the Negro Female Professionals." Phylon, 30 (Spring 1969), pp. 17-26.
> Discusses the Black professional women and concludes that Black women have more education than Black men. Therefore, because of their education, Black women have made relatively

(Bock, W. Wilbur)
greater contributions to the total number of Black professionals.

331   Bond, Jean C. and Perry, Pat. "Has the Black Man Been Castrated?" Liberator, 9 (May 1969), pp. 4-8.
Two Black women give their views of the Black man and how he sees the Black woman. They believe that the Black woman's place is beside her Black man, and not in front of or behind him.

332   Bonner, Florence. "Black Women and White Women: A Comparative Analysis of Perceptions of Sex Roles for Self, Ideal-Self and the Ideal-Male." The Journal of Afro-American Issues, (Summer 1974), pp. 237-246.
Attempts to examine whether the stereotype conceptions of the Black woman influence her attitude toward "traditional" sex-roles, and if that response is significantly different from the white female's perspective.

333   Boweles, Eva D. "Opportunities for the Educated Colored Woman." Opportunity, 1 (March 1923).
Discusses the various vocations for Black women: teaching, social work, nursing, medicine, business, and law. Also mentions a number of outstanding Black women: Sadie Mossell, Madam C. J. Walker, Mrs. Malone, and Maggie L. Walker.

334   Boyer, Sallie C. "Visit with Ethel Hedgeman Lyle: Founder of Alpha Kappa Alpha Sorority." The Brown American, (November-December 1941), pp. 18-19.
Discusses the events surrounding the founding of the AKA Sorority at Howard University in 1908.

335   Brawley, Benjamin G. "Phillis Wheatley." The Voice of the Negro, (January 1906).
A biographical sketch of the early life of poet Phillis Wheatley. Also discusses some of her poems.

336   Brewer, William M. "Mary McLeod Bethune." Negro History Bulletin, 19 (November 1955), p. 36.
A short biographical sketch of the great educator and women's rights leaders. Mary McLeod Bethune was a leader who rose from the strength of her great ability and the unquestioned choice of those whom she inspired and led as all leaders worthy of their commission have done.

337   _____. "Mary Church Terrell." The Negro History Bulletin, 18, (October 1954), p. 2.
A tribute to the great Black educator and woman's right advocate. Mrs. Terrell passed away in her ninety-first year on July 24, 1954.

338   Brooks, Gwendolyn. "Why Negro Women Leave Home." Negro
       Digest, 9 (March 1951), pp. 26-28.
          Contends that Black women demand dignity and respect and
       resent dollar dole-outs. Concludes that unless Blacks
       receive those things, they will increasingly prefer to live
       alone.

339   Brooks, Lillie. "I Didn't Raise My Boy to be a Fighter."
       Negro Digest. (February 1951), pp. 3-6.
          Ex-heavyweight champion, Joe Louis' mother, Lillie Brooks,
       says the happiest days of her life will be when her son lays
       down his gloves--for keeps.

340   Brown, Jean Collier. "The Economic Status of Negro Women."
       The Southern Workman, 60 (October 1931), pp. 430-431.
          A brief analysis of the economic status of Black women and
       factors of job discrimination based on race and six in the
       job market. Points out factors of discrimination in facto-
       ries, between white women workers and black women workers.
       Data gathered from 1930 census reports and published reports
       by the Women's Bureau.

341   Bruce, Josephine B. "What Has Education Done for Colored
       Women." The Voice of the Negro, (July 1904), pp. 294-298.
          Because of education Black women have risen to some emi-
       nence in the world, as teachers, leaders in philanthropic
       work, temperance advocates, church workers, and in many
       other lines of activity which require ability and endurance,
       education and character.

342   Burson, Leon. "Ma' Sutton of Auburn Avenue." Service, (July
       1951).
          About a Black woman who operated a cafe in Atlanta,
       Georgia for 32 years, 1918-1952.

343   Burroughs, Nannie H. "Not Color but Character." The Voice of
       the Negro, (July 1904), pp. 277-279.
          One day the standards may be raised higher and higher
       until the name "Black woman" will be synonymous with
       uprightness of character and loftiness of purpose. More-
       over, let character, and not color, be the first requisite
       to admission into any home, church or social circle, and a
       new day will begin for ten million people.

344   "Camilla Williams." Opportunity, (Winter 1947), pp. 42-43.
          Tells of the first Black to sing a woman's lead for the
       New York City Opera Company. A short biographical sketch of
       Miss Williams is included.

345   Campbell, E. Simms. "Are Black Women Beautiful?" Negro
       Digest, 9 (June 1951), pp. 16-20.

(Campbell, E. Simms).
Artist Campbell, who makes a living drawing beautiful women, says that dark skinned women are as beautiful as fair ones, and because of their color, they are excellent models.

346   Carnegie, Mary E. "The Impact of Integration on the Nursing Profession. An Historical Sketch." Negro History Bulletin, (April 1965), p. 154.
Mrs. Carnegie contends in the often painful process of achieving full integration, any minority suffers indignities, but prejudice in nursing is being exposed, indentified and dealt with.

347   _____. "Are Negro Schools of Nursing Needed Today?" Nursing Outlook, 12 (February 1964), pp. 53-56.
Black nursing schools are needed because even though most white nursing schools admit Black students, they make no overt actions to enroll or recruit Black students.

348   Carper, Laura. "The Negro Family and the Moynihan Report." Dissent, (March-April 1966).
Criticism of the Moynihan Report and its impact on Black people. The need for Black people to acquire social and economic power is the challenge.

349   Cartwright, Marguerite. "A New Star is Born: Charlotte Wesley Holloman." Negro History Bulletin, 18 (April 1954), pp. 153-154.
A short sketch of a Black woman soprano who won national acclaim while she was still young and attending Howard University.

350   _____. "Etta Moten: Glamorous Grandmother." Negro History Bulletin, 18 (March 1955), pp. 153-154.
A short sketch of a woman who combined her career as a singer and a mother. She was called by one writer--foremost singer-actress of her race, an inspiration, not only to the Negro, but to all human-kind.

351   Cavan, Ruth Shonie. "Negro Family Disorganization and Juvenile Delinquency." Journal of Negro Education, 28 (Summer 1959), pp. 230-239.
Discusses the Black mother as the central figure in the Black family. Concludes that the children see the mother as a model of the parent in the family.

352   Chappele, Yvonne, R. "The Black Women on the Negro College Campus." The Black Scholar, (January-February 1970), pp. 36-39.
The most important service the Black woman can render on campus in seeking to ease the frustration factor is simply to be a friend to her male colleague. The Black

(Chappele, Yvonne, R.)
woman on the Black college campus must also work hard to
make her institution progressive, innovative, and supportive
of the goals of Black people.

353 Chayer, Mary Ella. "Mary Eliza Mahoney." American Journal of
Nursing, 54 (1959), p. 429.
Miss Mahoney was the first Black who had the courage to
enter a school of nursing, side by side with her white
sisters, graduate, and become an outstanding student and
tender practitioner, an exemplary citizen, and an untiring
worker in both her local and national professional nursing
organizations.

354 Childress, Alice and others. "Remembrances of Eslanda
(Robeson)." Freedomways, 6 (Fall 1966), pp. 227-342.
Explores the life of the wife of the great actor-singer,
Paul Robeson. A number of people tell how they remembered
her. Mrs. Robeson died in New York City on December 13,
1965.

355 Chisholm, Shirley. "Race, Revolution and Women." Black
Scholar, (December 1971), pp. 17-20.
Mrs. Chisholm believes that women in this country must
become revolutionaries and that they must start in the
homes, schools, and churches. Women must work and fight for
the integration of male and female and human rights.

356 _____. "Racism and Anti-Feminism." The Black Scholar,
(January-February 1970), pp. 40-45.
America is both racist and anti-feminist and these two
things are the prime traditions of this country.

357 _____. "A Visiting Feminine Eye." McCall, (August 1970).
Mrs. Shirley Chisholm discusses the frustrations of sex
prejudice and comes to the conclusion that sex prejudice is
much harder to fight than racial prejudice.

358 "Citizen Extraordinary: Mary McLeod Bethune." The Brown
American, (Winter-Spring 1944), p. 5.
Article about Miss Bethune and her accomplishments over
the years, including her wartime achievements.

359 Clark, Alice. "Frances Ellen Watkins Harper." Negro History
Bulletin, 5 (January 1942), p. 83.
Article about the Black woman who is known as the first
Black American to attempt short story writing. Mrs. Harper
was born in 1825 and died in 1911.

360 Clarke, John Henrik. "The Black Woman: A Figure in World
History." Essence, (May 1971).

(Clarke, John Henrik)
Various references are made about Black women and their importance in world history. Discusses such Black women as the Black African queen, Cleopatra. It is probably because of the political implications of her love affair with the Roman, Mark Antony, that racist countries have insisted on painting Cleopatra white.

361   Cole, Johnnetta. "Black Women in America: An Annotated Bibliography." The Black Scholar, (December 1971), pp. 42-53.
By far the best annotated bibliography on Black women to date. This work also includes women in Africa and the Caribbean.

362   Congdon, T. B., Jr. "Ann Lowe, Society's Best Kept Secret: Only Negro American Dress Designer." Saturday Evening Post, (12 December 1964).
This article concerning the life of Ann Lowe, one of America's leading dress designers and Black. It points to the fact that few people know that Ann Lowe was Black which possibly could have accounted for much of her fame.

363   Conrad, Earl. "I Bring You General Tubman." The Black Scholar, 1 (January-February 1970).
The foremost authority on Harriet Tubman discusses her life and how she symbolizes the spiritual-material experience of her life, in all of her words, in the leadership she gave to the slave, in the inspiration she proved to the abolitionists, both white and Black, and in her total contribution to the Black-white national policy.

364   Crawford, Marc. "Should Marian Anderson Retire?" Ebony, (June 1960), pp. 77-81.
Music critics are divided on whether Miss Anderson should retire.

365   Crockett, Jacqueline. "An Essay on Gwendolyn Brooks." Negro History Bulletin, 19 (November 1955).
Written by a junior at Central State College, it tells of Miss Brook's life and accomplishments.

366   Dabney, Wendell P. "Maggie L. Walker: A Tribute to a Friend." Opportunity, 7 (July 1935), p. 216.
Discusses Mrs. Walker as one of Virginia's distinguished citizens, a bank president, a civic worker, and as probably one of the ablest American business women of this generation.

367   Dandridge, Dorothy. "Don't be Afraid of Sex Appeal." Ebony, (May 1952), pp. 24-30.

(Dandridge, Dorothy)
   Famous singer-actress discuss sex and says sex is more
mental and spiritual than physical. She also warns women
about too open a display of sex.

368 Davis, Angela. "Reflections on the Black Woman's Role in the
    Community of Slaves." The Black Scholar, (December 1971),
    pp. 2-15.
       Miss Davis surmises that the Black women of today must
    accept the full weight of a legacy wrought in blood by our
    mothers in chains. She concludes that our fight, while
    identical in spirit, reflects different conditions and thus
    implies different paths of struggle.

369 Davis, Lenwood G. "Black Women Contribute to History."
    Observer's Periscope, Special Edition of Portland/Oregon/Ob-
    server, (14 February 1974), p. 4.
       Discusses the contributions that Black women made to the
    United States during the Civil War, Reconstruction, and
    Post-Reconstruction era.

370 _____. "Historical First Facts of Black Women." Observer's
    Periscope, Special Edition of Portland/Oregon/Observer,
    (14 February 1974), p. 15.
       Discusses Black women who first accomplished a certain
    thing, e.i. first Black woman doctor, the first Black woman
    lawyer, the first Black woman judge, and so forth.

371 Deasy, Leila Calhoun and Quinn, Olive Westbrooke. "The Urban
    Negro and Adoption of Children." Child Welfare, New York:
    Child Welfare League of America, Inc., 41 (1962), pp. 400-
    407.
       Focuses on the attitudes of urban Blacks toward the
    adoption of children. Black couples were interviewed in
    Baltimore and Washington. The respondents think of adoption
    agencies as the prime source of adoptive children and ex-
    pressed no great fear of involvement with them.

372 Dunnigan, Alice E. "Early History of Negro Women in Journal-
    ism." Negro History Bulletin, 23 (Special Summer Issues
    1965), p. 178.
       Discusses seventeen Black women in journalism. There are
    several paragraphs about each woman.

373 _____. "The Success of Anne Jean Clore." Service, (January
    1951), pp. 7-10.
       A Black woman opened up a restaurant in Washington, D. C.
    for Blacks after World War II because of the constant influx
    of Black government workers into the Nation's Capital.

374 _____. "F. D. R. 's Last Meal." Service, (April 1951),
    pp. 15-17.

(Dunnigan, Alice E.)
  Tells of F. D. R. 's last meal prepared by his Black cook, Mrs. Daisy Bonner, White House cook for twenty years. Mrs. Bonner tells the events surrounding the president's last meal.

375 Ebert, Alan. "Aretha-Through the Eyes of Love." Essence, (December 1973), p. 38.
  A portrait of "Lady Soul," Aretha Franklin. There is also a discussion about her early childhood and her family.

376 _____. "A Song Named Roberta." Essence, (November 1974), p. 46.
  Article about singer Roberta Flack. Miss Flack talked about a number of topics, including Black women in show business. She concludes that all Black women in show business are potential victims. It's damn tough for a Black woman hanging out there on her own, surmised Miss Flack.

377 _____. "Melba." Essence, (July 1973), p. 28.
  A portrait of Melba Moore, "Another Lady Sings the Blues." Miss Moore was born on October 29, 1945. There is a discussion of Miss Moore's fight to climb to the top and become a successful actress and singer.

378 "Edith Irby Revisited." Ebony, (July 1963), pp. 52-59.
  About the first Black to graduate from a Southern (University of Arkansas) medical school. Dr. Edith Irby Jones graduated in 1948. This is a discussion about her as a successful doctor, wife, and mother.

379 Eggleston, Cecelia. "What a Negro Mother Faces." Forum, 100 (August 1938).
  Describes the frustrations and anxieties faced by the Black women attaining motherhood and consideration for factors of health and physical well-being, faith and future-goals and aspirations for the child.

380 Epstein, Cynthia Fuchs. "Black and Female: The Double Whammy." Psychology Today, (August 1973), p. 57.
  A study of Black professional women. Suggests that double discrimination can work in reverse. Edged on by supportive families, seen as less threatening than Black men, pushed by the feminist tide, some Black women are vaulting ahead despite the difficulties.

381 Farley, Reynolds. "Fertility Among Urban Blacks." The Milbank Memorial Fund Quarterly, Part 2 (April 1970), pp. 183-214.
  Discussion of the changing fertility rates among Black women in urban and rural areas and the factors influencing fertility. Upward social mobility, fecundity changes,

(Farley, Reynolds)
socio-economic variables, and biologic factors that are related to fertility.

382   Feger, H. V. "A Girl Who Became a Great Woman." Negro History Bulletin, 5 (March 1942), p. 123.
      Discussion of Lucy Laney, a Black woman who was a member of the first graduating class in 1873 at Atlanta University. Miss Laney opened a private school for Black children in Augusta, Georgia. Miss Laney died October 23, 1933.

383   Feinstein, Herbert. "Lena Horne Speaks Freely." Ebony, (May 1963), pp. 61-67.
      The world-famed singer and actress was interviewed by Mr. Feinstein and expressed her feelings about race-relations, marriage, and the stage.

384   Fleming, Beatrice J. "American's First Woman Bank President." Negro History Bulletin, 5 (January 1942), p. 75.
      This article is about a Black woman, Maggie L. Walker, who in 1903 organized the Saint Luke Penny Saving Bank, for the children of Richmond, Virginia, and became its first president.

385   Fleming, Walter Lynwood. "The Servant Problem in a Black Belt Village," Sewanee Review, (January 1905).
      Speaks to the problems that white plantation owners are experiencing in trying to maintain servants. The setting is Auburn, Alabama, 1903. Some of the problems are related to increased migration of Blacks to the northern cities, some Black housekeepers declaring the independence of Blacks and they also desire higher wages.

386   Foster, G. Allen. "The Woman Who Saved the Union Navy." Ebony, (July 1964), pp. 48-50.
      Mary Louvestre, a slave, helped defeat the Rebels in a crucial sea battle by spying on the South. Miss Louvestre copied secret drawings of the ship "Merrimac" during repeated visits to the chief engineer's office and then smuggled the secret drawings through Rebel ships and turned them over to the Union Army.

387   "Four in One: First Negro Woman to Head an American Embassy." Time, (28 May 1965).
      Gives a brief description of the nomination of Patricia Roberts Harris as the U. S. Ambassador to Luxembourg by President Johnson.

388   Fraizer, E. Franklin. "Ethnic Family Patterns: The Negro Family in the United States." American Journal of Sociology, 53 (May 1948), pp. 435-438.

(Fraizer, E. Franklin)
Feels that the loss of the African cultural heritage and the requirements of slavery caused the Black family to develop as a natural organization with the mother as head. Important differences in the organization of the family and its approximation to the American pattern are related to the emerging class structure.

389 _____. "New Role of the Negro Woman." Ebony, (August 1960), p. 46.
If the Black woman is true to her tradition of independence and self-assertion, she will not be satisfied with mere acceptance by white America but will join with the women of the world in the revolution which is creating a new world which will be free of colonialism, racial distinction and economic exploitation.

390 _____. "The Negro Slave Family." Journal of Negro History, 15 (April 1930), pp. 198-206.
Discusses the important role that the mother played in the slave family. Over a hundred sources were used to support the author's many interpretations of the slave family.

391 _____. "An Analysis of Statistics on Negro Illegitimacy in the United States." Social Forces, (1932), pp. 249-257.
An analysis of illegitimacy of Black people in all 48 states based on the author's own research and analysis of available statistical information in the records of the Departments of health and vital statistics. Conclusions suggests an upward trend of illegitimacy among Black families during the period of 1917 to 1928.

392 _____. "Problems and Needs of Negro Children and Youth Resulting From Family Disorganization." Journal of Negro Education, 19 (1950), pp. 269-277.
The family has become disorganized because the mother, and not the father, has played the major role in it.

393 Fuentes, Sonia. "Job Discrimination and the Black Woman." Crisis, (March 1970), pp. 103-108.
It is now up to the Black woman to use the available means to secure her rights, and up to the rest of the country to cooperate and assist her in her struggle for equality.

394 Furstenberg, Frank F. "Premarital Pregnancy Among Black Teenagers." Transaction, 7 (May 1970), pp. 52-55.
Article dealing with the question of premarital pregnancy among Black teenagers. Survey deals with questions relating to the acceptance of a first pregnancy out of wedlock, and attitudes toward illegitimacy among lower-class blacks. Ninety-six percent of the respondents interviewed were

(Furstenberg, Frank F.)
Black and results reveal the following characteristics:
1. 80% of the household heads were either unemployed or
held unskilled or service jobs. 2. 47% of the families
were headed by a female. 3. The median number of children
in the family was five, and nearly all the women were still
of childbearing age. 4. Over half the mothers had their
first child before they were 18 years old. 5. An illegitimate birth had already occurred in over half the families.

395 Gage, Nina D. and Hampt, Alma C. "Some Observations on Negro
Nursing in the South." Public Health Nursing, 24 (1932),
pp. 674-680.
Discussion on the problems facing Black nurses in the
South. Black women were denied a good basic secondary
education, so necessary for their admission to the better
schools of nursing. Black nurses, however well qualified,
were still being barred from many offering advance courses
in nursing education. Because of the many community problems of Blacks, the Black nurses often had to serve as
community leaders. It was generally the Black nurse who
approached prejudiced health officials in order to get
needed health facilities for Black people.

396 Garland, Phyl. "Builders of a New South." Ebony, (August
1966), pp. 27-37.
Black heroines of Dixie play major role in challenging
racist traditions. A number of Black women who are helping
to change the South are included.

397 ____. "Gwendolyn Brooks: Poet Laureate." Ebony, (July
1968), pp. 48-57.
Shows how fame has not tarnished Miss Brooks' basic
simplicity and utter lack of pretension.

398 Gayles, J. N. Jr. "Health Brutality and the Black Life Cycle."
Black Scholar, 5 (May 1974), pp. 2-9.
Various references are made to Black women, especially as
mothers. As many as one-third to one-half of Black women
who are delivered in public hospitals have no prenatal care,
and it goes without saying that the many hundred that are
delivered in crowded apartment rooms have neither prenatal
care nor delivery hygenics. As a result, neither Black
babies nor Black mothers have a strong chance of survival.

399 Genovese, Eugene. "The Slave Family, Women—A Reassessment of
Matriarchy, Emasculation, Weakness." Southern Voices,
(August-September 1974), pp. 9-16.
Attempts to clear up many of the myths of the Black woman
and families. Concludes that slave families and Southern
Black families after the Civil War were remarkably stable;
that Black women during and after slavery were supportive

(Genovese, Eugene)
   of their Black men; and that Black man and wife were close
   to today's ideal of individual strength and development.

400   Gloster, Hugh M. "Zola Neal Hurston, Novelist and Folk-
      lorist." Phylon, 4 (1943), pp. 153-159.
         A biographical sketch of Miss Hurston's life and literary
      career. Concludes that Miss Hurston's major works represent
      a unique amalgam of folklore and fiction.

401   Golden, Bernett. "Black Women's Liberation." Essence,
      (February 1974), p. 36.
         Surmises that Black women want Black men to assert their
      rights as fiercely as they do theirs, a task which will re-
      quire courage and understanding. Black women must redefine
      "womanhood" and grow along with Black men.

402   Greene, Marjorie. "Ann Petry Planned to Write." Opportunity,
      24 (April-June 1946), pp. 78-79.
         An article about Miss Petry, who won a $2400 literary
      fellowship for her first novel, The Street. A short bio-
      graphical sketch is included.

403   Gullattee, Alyce C. "Psychiatric Factors to Consider in Re-
      search on the Black Women." The Journal of Afro-American
      Issues, 2 (Summer 1974), pp. 199-203.
         Discusses several areas concerning Black women which need
      more research. Some of the areas are: depression, alco-
      holism, ego, anxiety, etc. Black women, and men, should
      share their knowledge and experience with the young.

404   Hansberry, Lorraine. "The Complex of (Black) Womanhood."
      Ebony, (August 1960), p. 46.
         For three centuries Black women have been the special
      victims of lust of brutes. Yet, they survived and gave a
      whole people a sense of survival. Moreover, Black women
      should never accept the notion of "your place."

405   Harlowe, Marie. "Sojourner Truth, The First Sit-In." Negro
      History Bulletin, 29 (Fall 1966), pp. 173-174.
         Sojourner Truth sat in the office of President Lincoln
      until he heard her suggestions for handling some problems
      concerning the avalanche of freed, unemployed slaves. A
      short biographical sketch of Miss Truth's life and activi-
      ties is included. Miss Truth died November 26, 1883, in
      Battle Creek, Michigan.

406   Hartnick, Allen. "Catherine Ferguson, Black Founder of a
      Sunday School." Negro History Bulletin, 35 (December 1972),
      pp. 176-177.
         Catherine Ferguson founded an early Sunday School in New
      York which sought to provide the poor with the basic

(Hartnick, Allen)
rudiments of an education. This school was started around
1814. Miss Ferguson was born 1779 and died 1854.

407   Hawkins, Mildred. "Negro Adoption-Challenge Accepted."
Child Welfare, New York: Child Welfare League of America,
Inc., 39 (December 1960), pp. 22-28.
Discusses the problems encountered with finding adoptive
parents for Black children. Several problems discussed
related to the increasing need for homes, the community
interpretation of adoption, the techniques used to stimulate
interest in adopting.

408   Haynes, Elizabeth Ross. "Negroes in Domestic Service in the
United States." Journal of Negro History, 8 (October 1923),
pp. 384-389.
A discussion on the role played by Blacks in the changes
and developments of domestic service in the United States
between 1893 and 1923. Also shows to some extent the
relation of Black domestic workers to white workers and some
of the larger problems in this field of employment.

409   _____. "Two Million Negro Women at Work." The Southern Workman, 51 (February 1922), pp. 64-72.
Analysis of Black Women in the three largest occupations
in which they are engaged: 1) domestic and personal
service, 2) agriculture, and 3) manufacturing and mechan-
ical industries.

410   Henderson, Edwin B. "Negro Women in Sports." Negro History
Bulletin, 15 (December 1951), p. 55.
Discusses women and girls in sports and concludes that so
long as women of other races and other nations engage in
sports with no proven evidence of detriment, Black girls
should also compete in sports.

411   Hepburn, D. "Edith Sampson Speaks for America." Our World,
6 (February 1951). pp. 24-29.
Edith Spurlock Sampson was the first Black to be named to
the United Nations and is an advocate of policy supporting
America's interest.

412   Herrick, Genevieve H. "Queen Mary: Champion of Negro Women."
Negro Digest, 9 (December 1950), pp. 32-39.
Mary McLeod Bethune at age 75 still continues to wage an
unceasing fight for Blacks.

413   Hertz, Hilda. "Unmarried Negro Mothers in Southern Urban Community." Social Forces, 23 (October 1944), pp. 73-79.
A survey of the attitudes toward illegitimacy among Black
people in Southern states show a variance from complete con-
demnation to acceptance. Information was obtained from the

(Hertz, Hilda)
pregnant women, their families, and members of the community. Methods used include informal interviews, casual
conversation and observation.

414   Herzog, Elizabeth. "Unmarried Mothers: Some Question to be
Answered and Some Answers to be Questioned." Child Welfare,
41 (October 1962), pp. 339-350.
Focuses on the problem of illegitimate births and unmarried mothers. Attention is focused on three main questions:
(1) How big is the problem (2) Who are the unmarried
mothers? and (3) What factors contribute to or are associated with births out of wedlock?

415   _____. "Is There a Breakdown of the Negro Family?" Social
Work, (January 1966), pp. 3-10.
Focuses on the controversy centered around Black families,
and discusses (1) whether the black family is "crumbling"
at a disastrous rate (2) whether the amount of breakdown
that exists is primarily due to poverty, or to cultural
inheritance, or to a cycle of self-perpetrating pathology
and (3) whether the remedy is to be sought primarily
through improving the economic, social and legal status of
Blacks or primarily through conducting a remedial campaign
aimed directly at the Black family.

416   _____. "Some Assumptions about the Poor." Social Review,
37: pp. 389-401.
Discusses the relevancy or irrelevancy of three assumptions about lower income individuals: (1) there is a
culture of poverty (2) the family and sex patterns of the
poor differ from those of the middle-class (3) the family
and sex patterns of poor blacks differ from those of whites
on the same socio-economic level.

417   _____. "Occupational Classes Among Negroes in Cities."
American Journal of Sociology, 35 (March 1930), pp. 718-
738.
Discusses the movement of Blacks in occupational classes
from the time of the Civil War. In Chicago the lower
occupational groups tend to concentrate in the transition
area of the city along the railroad tracks. In an area with
a large concentration of the upper occupational classes the
efforts of these classes to escape from the areas occupied
by the lower economic groups in order to maintain their own
standards of behavior is greatly accelerated.

418   Himes, Joseph. "The Assessment of Adjustment of Aged Negro
Women in a Southern City." Phylon, 23: 139-147.
Report of an exploratory study designed to assess the
adjustment of aged Black women in a Southern (Durham,
N. C.) urban community. Concludes that the women exhibited

(Himes, Joseph)
the greatest social adequacy in managing the holdhouse, social participation, and personal decisions, and the least in respect to exclusion from leadership roles.

419   Holmes, Jean Baxter. "That Future Days Shall Be Different." The Brown American, (Spring-Summer 1942), pp. 7-8.
About Black women and how they supported World War II in the hope that after the war was over Black women and men would be treated with respect.

420   Horton, Luci. "The Distaff Side of Politics: Black Elected Female Office Holders Double in Four Years." Ebony, (December 1973), pp. 48-54.
Black women only hold about 337 of the more than 520,000 elected offices in the United States. Photos of most of the major women office holders in America are included.

421   _____. "The Three-Horned 'Dilemma' Facing Negro Women." Ebony, (August 1966), pp. 118-123.
The three dilemmas are: rapport with Black men, the lowly poor, and white women.

422   _____. "The Legacy of Phillis Wheatley." Ebony, (March 1974), pp. 94-102.
Most of America's leading Black women poets honor America's first Black woman of letters at Mississippi festival.

423   Hundley, Mary S. "The National Association of Colored Women." Opportunity, (Journal of Negro Life), (June 1925), p. 185.
Discusses the origin, purpose, and history of the development of the National Association of Colored Women.

424   Hunter, Charlayne. "Blacks and the Liberation Movement." Black Politician, 2 (January 1971), p. 15.
Discusses the women's liberation movement and it's relationship to Black women. Includes interviews with Frances Beal, Third World Alliances; Mrs. Eleanor Holmes Norton, chairman of city's Commission on Human Rights; and Mrs. Shirley Lacy, training director for Scholarship, Education and Defense Fund for Racial Equation. Conclude that the problems of Black women are related more to blackness than to status as women.

425   Hunton, Addie. "Negro Womanhood Defended." The Voice of the Negro, (July 1904), pp. 280-282.
The Black woman with her deeper interest in her people, her larger knowledge of their needs, with the culture and character that education give, is constantly at work for the uplift of her race.

426   Hymen, Herbert H. and Reed, John Shelton. "Black Matriarchy
       Reconsidered: Evidence from Secondary Analysis of Sample
       Surveys." Public Opinion Quarterly, 33 (Summer 1969),
       pp. 346-54.
          Two distinct notions embody the concept of "Black matri-
       archy." 1) Some proportion of Black households are headed
       by women, and 2) even in intact Black families, the wives
       exercise predominant influence over family affairs.

427   Jackson, Jacquelyne J. "But Where are the Men?" Black
       Scholar, (December 1971), pp. 30-41.
          Ultimately, Black women must be concerned with the reso-
       lution of the issue of an insufficient supply of males, and
       aid in developing means of increasing that supply.

428   Jackson, Mahalia. "Marital Bliss vs Single Blessedness."
       Ebony, (April 1968), pp. 89-100.
          Article about the famous gospel singer, who was married
       twice and divorced twice, and who is giving advice to other
       women facing a life of loneliness.

429   James, Milton M. "Laura Wheeler Waring." Negro History
       Bulletin, 19 (March 1956), pp. 126-128.
          A survey of the life of a great Black woman painter and
       artist. Miss Waring was born in 1887 in Hartford, Conn.
       and died on February 3, 1948.

430   Jeffers, Trellie. "The Black Woman and the Black Middle
       Class: A Personal Viewpoint." Black Scholar, 4 (March-
       April 1973), pp. 37-41.
          The future of Black America calls the Black woman to the
       battle post that she has always occupied, that is, the
       position of supreme moral leadership, even though that
       leadership was implicit. Mrs. Jeffers concludes that the
       Black woman is now called upon to assume side by side with
       her brother, the post of EXPLICIT moral leadership, in order
       that the Black masses may win the decisive victory which
       will be ours.

431   Johnson, Clifton H. "Mary Ann Shadd: Crusader for the Free-
       dom of Man." Crisis, (April-May 1971), pp. 89-90.
          A brief biographical sketch of the first Black woman to
       edit a newspaper in North America. Miss Shadd established
       the "Provincial Freeman" in 1854.

432   Jones, Anna H. "A Century's Progress of the American Colored
       Woman," The Voice of Negro, (September 1905), pp. 631-633.
          Black women have made a number of accomplishments over the
       past century especially as: teachers, inventors, lawyers,
       stenographers, bookkeepers, saleswomen, dressmakers,
       caterers, hairdressers, milliners, etc.

433   Jones, Anna H. "The American Colored Woman." The Voice of
       the Negro, (October 1905), pp. 692-694.
          Black woman of tomorrow will take advantage of the oppor-
       tunities for industrial and intellectual development just
       as the Black woman of today (1905) is doing, just as the
       Black woman of the past has done.

434   Jones, Vickie. "Divorce: Two Women Who Experienced It."
       Essence, (April 1974), pp. 52,53,95.
          Two women discuss their experiences as divorcees. They
       talk about the problems that a Black woman alone faces and
       the adjustments that must be made.

435   Kamii, Constance. "Class Differences in the Socialization
       Practices of Negro Mothers." Journal of Marriage and the
       Family, 29 (May 1967), pp. 302-310.
          Class differences in the socialization practices of Black
       mothers were investigated in the context of their child-
       rearing goals. Direct observation of mother-child inter-
       actions in the homes and a card-sorting method of studying
       child-rearing goals led to the conclusion that middle and
       lower-lower class Black mothers do not differ fundamentally
       in their goals, but they differ considerably in their
       socialization practices. The relationship of these prac-
       tices to the development of analytic identification,
       internal controls, and subsequent conformity to society's
       norms was discussed, along with the implications of these
       conclusions for education.

436   Kanno, Nellie B. "Comparative Life Styles of the Black Female
       in the United States and the Black Female in Lesotho."
       The Journal of Afro-American Issues, 2 (Summer 1974),
       pp. 212-217.
          Discusses the life styles of Black women from two differ-
       ent cultures. The twin "adversities" of being both female
       and Black have produced a group of women determined to
       succeed in societies which practice the most blatant form of
       oppression and in which it is assumed that the Black female
       presides over a family structure which is undergoing pro-
       gressive deterioration.

437   Katz, Maude White. "She Who Would be Free-Resistance."
       Freedomway, 2 (Winter 1962), pp. 60-70.
          Describes the possessions of Black women from slavery to
       present and how they resisted and are still resisting their
       oppression. Also states that Black women have influenced
       Black men to also resist the "establishment over the years.

438   _____. "The Negro Woman and the Law." Freedomways, 2
       (Summer 1962), pp. 278-86.
          Reviews the historical relationship between the Black
       woman and the law. Concludes that a radical change in law

74

(Katz, Maude White)
and custom is urgent and necessary to right the wrongs
against the Negro woman.

439   Kellor, Frances A. "Opportunities for Southern Negro Women in
      Northern Cities." The Voice of the Negro, (July 1905),
      pp. 470-473.
         There are many kinds of opportunities for Black women from
      the South in Northern cities. Points out the many different
      associations and organizations formed to protect Black
      women in the North.

440   _____. "Southern Colored Girls in the North." Charities,
      (18 March 1905).
         Deals with the problem of unemployment of the Black women
      in New York City, and the need to have some form of pro-
      tection for Black women from northern whites who seek a form
      of slave labor for their homes.

441   King, Helen. "The Black Woman and Women's Lib." Ebony,
      (March 1971), pp. 68-76.
         Black females believe that they should stand behind Black
      men and not against them. In other words, the Women's
      Liberation movement is taking away the time and energy of
      Black women.

442   King, Karl. "Adolescent Perception of Power Structure in the
      Negro Family." Journal of Marriage and the Family, 31
      (November 1969), pp. 751-755.
         The purpose of this study was to access the perception of
      Black adolescents concerning the power structure within the
      Negro family. The sample was divided by the father's
      occupation into three levels: white collar, blue collar and
      unskilled. The results indicated the male and female
      adolescents viewed the power structure to be mainly syn-
      cratic. Males reported stronger father participation than
      did the females, and females reported stronger mother par-
      ticipation than did the males. Both males and females
      indicated stronger father participation in decision-making
      than has been historically presented.

443   King, Mae C. "The Politics of Sexual Stereotypes." Black
      Scholar, 4 (March-April 1973), pp. 12-23.
         The stereotyped images of the Black woman discussed are:
      The "non-feminist", the "depreciated sex object", and the
      "loser image". These stereotypes are in turn complemented
      by what appears to be otherwise general policy of invis-
      ibility by the mass media with respect to Black women.

444   Kitt, Eartha. "The Most Exciting Men in My Life." Ebony,
      (January 1953), pp. 26-36.
         Most of the men Miss Kitt mentions are white, from Orson
      Welles to Michelle De Merbe.

445   Knighten, Grace. "I Was a Lady-in Waiting." Negro Digest,
      (September 1951), pp. 53-57.
          For over five years, 1909-1914, a Black woman from
      Chicago was a member of the royal household of India's
      Maharajah of Tikari.

446   "Lady Racketters: New Crime Menace." Ebony, (June 1952),
      pp. 46-50.
          Article about Black women racketeers. Twelve of the
      biggest Black women racketeers are discussed along with
      photos of them.

447   Lang, F. "Sick Cell and the Pill: Birth Control Pills Dan-
      gerous to Black Woman," Ramparts, (February 1972).
          Points to the dangers for Black women with sickle cell
      anemia or the sicklē cell trait who take the birth control
      pill. Recent articles in medical journals suggest that
      women with sickle cell anemia or the sickle cell trait may
      be likely to develop blood clots if they take oral contra-
      ceptives.

448   Latimer, Catherine. "Catherine Ferguson." Negro History
      Bulletin, 5 (November 1941), pp. 38-39.
          About the first Black to establish a Sunday School in New
      York City about 1800. Miss Ferguson died of cholera in New
      York City, July 11, 1854, at age about seventy-five.

449   Laurent, Philip St. "The Negro in World History: Part 73,
      Mary McLeod Bethune," Tuesday Magazine, (May 1973), pp.
      12-14.
          A discussion of Miss Bethune's life and her stress on edu-
      cation. Miss Bethune believed that education was the great
      American adventure, the largest public enterprise in the
      United States, and the country's most important business.

450   _____, "The Negro in World History: Part 70, Bessie
      Coleman." Tuesday Magazine, (January 1973), pp. 10-12.
          About the first licensed Black woman pilot in the entire
      world. Miss Coleman acquired her pilot's license in Paris,
      France in 1922 from the Federation Aeronautique Interna-
      tionale.

451   Lewis, Mollie V. "Negro Women in Steel." The Crisis, 45,
      (February 1938), p. 54.
          Article about Black women working in steel mills in Gary,
      Indiana and how they must work together with whites to
      demand higher wages.

452   "Life of Mary McLeod Bethune." Our World, 5 (December 1950),
      pp. 32-35.
          Article on the great educator and human rights advocate.

453   Manning, Seaton W. "The Changing Negro Family: Implications
      for the Adoption of Children." Child Welfare, New York:
      Child Welfare League of America, Inc., 43 (1964).
         Discussion on the assumptions of sociologists that the
      number of Black adoptive parent applications would increase
      as Black families moved upward on the socio-economic scale
      from lower-class and working-class statuses to middle-class
      rank. However, this was not the case and the discussion
      centers around the crucial question of why?

454   Mapp, Edward. "Black Women in Films." Black Scholar, 4
      (March-April 1973), pp. 42-46.
         Dr. Mapp surmises that the Black woman's film image has
      been defined by others rather than by herself. The result
      is a tragic history of stereotyping and a steady procession
      of mammies, maids, miscegenists, matriarchs, madams, and
      assorted "Made-it-for-money" types.

455   March, Stephen. "Elizabeth Cotten, Gentle Genius of the
      Guitar." Southern Voices, (August-September 1974),
      pp. 69-72.
         Tells of a Black woman Elizabeth Cotten, born in Chapel
      Hill, N. C., 71 years ago. When she was 11 years old, she
      made up a song about the trains that passed through Chapel
      Hill. Recognition of her talent came late and royalties for
      "Freight Train" have passed her by.

456   "Matriarch." Time, (22 July 1946).
         Gives a brief description of the work being done by Mary
      McLeod Bethune. Mary came from a West African matriarchal
      tribe where the women led their men around by the nose.

457   Matson, R. Lynn. "Phillis Wheatley--Soul Sister?" Phylon,
      33 (Fall 1972), pp. 222-230.
         While not particularly race conscious or a protestor of
      slavery Mrs. Wheatley cannot be dismissed, as she has been,
      on the grounds that she abandoned her race and completely
      assimilated into the slave society. If she is not exactly
      a soul sister, she is certainly a distant relative.

458   McBroom, Patricia. "The Black Matriarchy: Healthy or Patho-
      logical?" Science News, 94 (October 1968).
         Focuses attention on the Moynihan Report. Black sociolo-
      gists say the Black families may not be the cause of social
      disintegration that whites have claimed but a healthy adap-
      tation to ghetto conditions.

459   McCrorey, Mary Jackson. "Lucy Laney." Crisis, (June 1934),
      p. 161.
         About Lucy Laney, who was principal of Haines Institute,
      Augusta, Georgia.

460   "Monica Mais is Her Name." Opportunity, 26 (October-December
       1948), p. 134.
         Autobiographical sketch of a young Black woman who became
       a coloratura soprano and could demand $1,000 and up per
       night for a concert. Miss Mais was called "a coloratura
       without equal in this (her) generation."

461   Morrison, Allan. "(Black) Women in the Arts." Ebony, (August
       1966), pp. 90-94.
        Since the American Revolution, Black women have proved
       their greatness in poetry, music, dance and sculpture. A
       number of Black women who contributed to the arts are
       named.

462   _____. "Mother Role Brings Broadway Fame." Ebony,
       (May 1960), pp. 97-104.
        On Claudia McNeil's performance as the matriarchal Lena
       Younger in Lorraine Hansberry's award-winning drama, A
       Raisin in the Sun.

463   "Mrs. Architect, Norma Merrick Fairweather; First Negro Woman
       to Graduate from Columbia University's School of Architec-
       ture." Our World, 5 (November 1960), pp. 57-59.
        About Norma Merrick Fairweather, the first Black woman to
       graduate from Columbia University's School of Architecture.

464   "Mrs. Bethune: Springarn Medalist." Crisis, (July 1935),
       p. 202.
        A sketch of Mary McLeod Bethune, winner of the NAACP
       Springarn Medal for 1934.

465   "Mrs. Buchanan Goes to Albany; For New York's First Negro
       Woman Legislator, Life in the State Capital is Complex,
       Very Fascinating." Our World, 10 (May 1955), pp. 50-53.
        Bessie Allison was the first Black woman to be elected to
       the New York State Assembly from New York's 12th Assembly.
       Mrs. Buchanan won the election in 1954.

466   "Mrs. Madaline Williams Honored." Crisis, 65 (June-July
       1958), pp. 364-367.
        The Honorable Madaline A. Williams was the first Black
       woman in the history of New Jersey to be elected an
       assembly-woman. Mrs. Williams was elected in November, 1957
       to represent Essex County in the state legislature.

467   Murray, Anna E. "The Negro Woman." Southern Workman, 33
       (April 1904), p. 232-234.
        Criticizes the article written by Eleanor Taylor and pub-
       lished in the January issue of the "Outlook". Tells of the
       efforts on the part of the Black woman to make the home as
       comfortable as possible despite the socio-economic factors
       that are constantly working against her.

468   Myers, Lena Wright. "Mothers from Families of Orientation as
       Role Models for Black Women." Northwest Journal of African
       and Black American Studies, 2 (Winter 1974), pp. 7-9.
         Briefly examines some literature which has possibly con-
       tributed to a misunderstanding of role models via the pro-
       cess of socialization for Black women. Also offers a brief
       review of some of the generalizations made by researchers
       who have utilized the traditional white model of evaluation
       and have suggested negative consequences for the Black woman
       as a result of "inadequate role models" from their families
       of orientation.

469   "National Association of Colored Women's Clubs." Southern
       Workman, (December 1922), pp. 543-545.
         Discusses the thirteenth biennial meeting of the National
       Association of Colored Women's Club, held in Richmond, Va.
       Discussion topics focused on the issues of the Dyer Anti-
       Lynching Bill, the industrial conditions in factories for
       women and the restoration of the home of Frederick Douglass.

470   "Negro Women in Skilled Defense Jobs." Monthly Labor Review,
       (November 1943).
         Gives statistics for Black women employed in the Navy Yard
       in Washington. Program of employment was sponsored by the
       National Youth Administration.

471   Ottley, Roi. "What's Wrong with Negro Women." Negro Digest,
       9 (December 1950), pp. 71-74.
         Concludes that what's wrong with Black women, has to do
       with Blacks, males and females. Both Black men and women
       are victims of a system which cripples aspiration.

472   "Outstanding Women Doctors." Ebony, (May 1964), pp. 68-70.
         Gives a brief history of Black women doctors, including
       several present day ones. There are only about 300 Black
       women doctors out of 13,000 women doctors in the United
       States.

473   Parkhurst, Jessie. "The Role of the Black Mammy in the Plan-
       tation Household." Journal of Negro History, 23 (July
       1938), pp. 349-369.
         Points out that the "Black Mammy" played one of the most
       important roles in the plantation household and that her
       influence in it has been underestimated.

474   Parrish, Milton. "Black Woman's Guide to the Black Man."
       Essence, (April 1974), p. 56.
         Attempts to tell Black women what they need to do to keep
       Black men happy.

475   "Philippa Duke Schryler." The Crisis, (May 1950) p. 276.
         About the Black teenage genius pianist and how she made
       triumphant tours in the deep South, and the West Indies.

476   Pierce, Pochida. "Divorce and the Negro Woman." Ebony,
       (July 1967), pp. 84-92.
          Concludes that whether or not the many problems facing the
       Black woman as a wife and divorcee will ever be solved, de-
       pends in large measure upon society's willingness to educate
       the Black male, employ him at jobs commensurate of self-
       worth. This would hasten the end of the Black matriarchal
       system.

477   _____. "Lena Horne at 51." Ebony, (July 1968), p. 125.
          Discusses Miss Horne's accomplishments over the years.
       Miss Horne has been in show business for 38 years.

478   _____. "The Mission of Marian Wright." Ebony, (June 1966),
       pp. 94-108.
          Tells of a young Black woman lawyer who gave up a soft
       life for Civil Rights crusade in Mississippi. She was the
       first Black woman to pass the state bar examination in 1965.

479   _____. "The Problem of the Negro Woman Intellectual."
       Ebony, (August 1966).
          Contends that the Black woman intellectual is misunder-
       stood. Concludes that as the Black Woman intellectual puts
       the past in perspective and accepts the challenges of the
       present and future, whatever problem she has, will probably
       be those of any intellectual. Some will be imagined, others
       real, including the constant search for truth in a society
       guided more by expediency than integrity.

480   Porter, Dorothy B. "Maria Louis Baldwin." Journal of Negro
       Education, (Winter 1952), pp. 94-96.
          Miss Baldwin was born in Cambridge, Massachusetts, on
       September 13, 1856. She was an educator and one of the
       "best school teachers" in the United States, regardless of
       color. Miss Baldwin died January 9, 1922.

481   _____. "Sarah Parker Remond, Abolitionist and Physician."
       Journal of Negro History, 20 (July 1935), pp. 287-293.
          About the great Black abolitionist, Sarah Parker Remond.
       Discusses her travels in Europe, where she received the
       degree of Doctor of Medicine in Florence, Italy in 1871.

482   Porter, Sylvia. "Negro Women and Poverty." San Francisco
       Chronicle, (5 August 1969), p. 48.
          Discussion of Black women and poverty. Statistics given
       point out that Black women sit on the bottom of the economic
       ladder, that the jobless rate for Black women is twice as
       high as the white woman and three times as high as the white
       man.

483   Powell, Hazel Scott. "I Found God in Show Business." Ebony,
       (May 1956), pp. 40-46.

(Powell, Hazel Scott)
   The wife of Adam Clayton Powell, Jr. sees no disagreement between religion and night club world.

484   Radin, Norma and Kandi, Constance K. "The Child-Rearing Attitudes of Disadvantaged Negro Mothers and Some Educational Implications." Journal of Negro Education, 34, (Spring 1965), pp. 138-146.
   A study of Black mothers' child-rearing attitudes. Concludes that there is much that educational institutions can do to help lower-class, Negro mothers alter some of their self-defeating child-rearing techniques.

485   Radin, Norman and Blasser, Paul H. "The Use of Parental Attitude Questionnaires with Culturally Disadvantaged Families." Journal of Marriage and the Family, 27 (August 1965), pp. 373-383.
   Discussion of some of the difficulties relating to administration and data interpretation when researchers employ parental attitude questionnaires with culturally disadvantaged families. Examines problems of language complexity, and differences in class and race between interviewers and respondents.

486   "Rarest Breed of Women: Black Businesswomen in the Executive Suites." Times, (8 November 1971), pp. 98-102.
   Discusses the Black businesswomen as the rarest breed of women and interviews several prominent Black businesswomen, including Barbara Edwards, vice-president of California's Northwestern Title Co.; Victoria Lynn Sanders, Chicago's only Black woman stockbroker, and several more.

487   Reed, Julia. "Marriage and Fertility in Black Female Teachers." The Black Scholar, 1 (January-February 1970), pp. 22-28.
   Based on research by the author on Black women teachers. Several conclusions are drawn. First, Black female teachers are more likely to marry, relative to white female teachers. Second, Black female teachers are more likely to experience broken marriages.

488   Reiner, Beatrice. "The Real World of the Teenage Negro Mother." Child Welfare, 47 (1968), pp. 391-396.
   Focuses attention on the "problem" of "illegitimate" births among Black teenage girls. It was found that unwed mothers who keep their babies come largely from poor and deprived environments that foster the development of this calamity and stifle opportunities for positive help for mother, father and child.

489   Reiss, Ira L. "Premarital Sexual Permissiveness Among Negroes and Whites." American Sociological Review, 29 (October 1964), pp. 688-689.

(Reiss, Ira L.)
Discussion of results from a sample of 903 students and 1,515 adults indicated that Blacks and whites differ considerably in the ways in which premarital sexual attitudes are produced and maintained.

490   Richards, Agnes. "The Black Swan." Negro Digest, (November 1950) p. 73-75.
The portrait of Elizabeth Taylor Greenfield, a slave girl born in 1809, who once sang at Buckingham Palace for Queen Victoria. Miss Greenfield was given the musical sobriquet the "Black Swan."

491   Riessman, Frank. "Low-Income Culture: The Strengths of the Poor." Journal of Marriage and the Family, 26 (November 1964), pp. 417-421.
A critique of the Moynihan report. Concludes that "the basic defect in the Moynihan thesis is a one-sided presentation of the consequences of segregation and discrimination."

492   Ritter, E. Jay. "Sojourner Truth." Negro History Bulletin, 26 (May 1963), p. 254.
Tells of the great Black woman, Sojourner Truth, and her meeting with President Lincoln on a morning in October, 1864.

493   Robinson, Fannie. "I Remember Bojangles." Ebony, (February 1953), pp. 49-50.
The wife of the famous dancer-actor, Bill "Bojangles" Robinson tells how after twenty years of marriage, separation and death she still loves Bill Robinson.

494   Robinson, Louise. "Dorothy Dandridge: Hollywood's Tragic Engima." Ebony, (March 1966), pp. 70-82.
Discusses Miss Dandridge's death on September 8, 1965 and concludes that the ill-fated star defies scrutiny even in death.

495   Sampson, Edith S. "I Like America." Negro Digest, (December 1950), pp. 3-8.
The first Black American delegate to the United Nations tells why she likes her country, but does not gloss over the handicaps and inequalities which Black people face in America.

496   Samuel, Nadene and Laird, Dorothy S. "The Self Concepts of Two Groups of Black Female College Students." Journal of Negro Education, 63 (Spring 1974), pp. 228-233.
Compares seven dimensions of self concept of Black females on a predominantly white campus with those on a predominantly Black campus. Concludes that the Black female

(Samuel, Nadene and Laird, Dorothy S.)
college student may not have as negative a self-image as one
may suppose, particularly if the Black female selects a university which has a large white population. There is also
the possibility that higher education may provide opportunities for Black females to see themselves more positively, to
become more than a "sexually convenient animal," thereby
overcoming some of the negative aspects which they have
assumed in the past.

497   Sanders, Charles L. "Lady Didn't Always Sing the Blues."
     Ebony, (January 1973), pp. 110-115.
     About Billie Holiday and the woman behind the legend.
     Three friends recall what Miss Holiday was like.

498   _____. "Radicialization of Angela Davis." Ebony, (July
     1971), pp. 114, 120.
     Discusses how Miss Davis' philosophy changed over the
     years. Contends that Birmingham, Alabama was the roots, but
     the radicalization of Angela Davis was hastened by what she
     heard and saw and began thinking about in Paris, France.

499   _____. "Requiem for 'Queen Dinah'." Ebony, (March 1964),
     pp. 146-154.
     Discusses Dinah Washington, often called "Queen of the
     Blues." Miss Washington died on December 14, 1963.

500   Sayre, Helen B. "Negro Women in Industry." Opportunity,
     (Journal of Negro Life), 2 (August 1924), pp. 242-244.
     A discussion of the various industries that Black women
     women are working in. Concludes that the Black woman's
     sudden entrance into industry is a new adventure and a
     dramatic innovation.

501   Schmelz, Annie M. "A Presbyterian Conference for Colored
     Women." Southern Workman, 54 (September 1925), p. 416.
     A summary of the Fifth Annual Conference for Colored
     Women held in Virginia under the auspices of the Women's
     Auxiliary of the Synod of Virginia of the Southern Presby-
     terian Church. Discussion centered around: (1) taking a
     religious census of the community, (2) establish daily
     Vacation Bible Schools, (3) organize bible classes and es-
     tablish family altars, (4) organize Parent-Teacher Associa-
     tions, (5) to seek greater harmony between different classes
     of Blacks, and (6) to request Black teachers to teach Negro
     history.

502   Schickel, R. "Leontyne Price: From Mississippi to the Met."
     Look, (17 January 1961), pp. 88-90.
     Concerns efforts on the part of Leontyne Price to sing in
     the Metropolitan Opera.

503   "Scientist Named 'Young Woman of the Year' by Mademoiselle
       Magazine." Negro History Bulletin, 16 (March 1953), p. 128.
          Dr. Jane Cook Wright of Harlem Hospital in New York is
       discussed. Dr. Wright was named "Young Woman of the Year"
       because of her outstanding contribution to medical science
       in the area of evaluations on the efficacy of drugs in can-
       cer treatment.

504   Scott, Emmett Jay. "Maggie J. Murray Washington (Mrs. Booker
       Taliaferro Washington): Part in Her Husband's Work."
       Ladies Home Journal, 24 (May 1907).
          Describes the part that Mrs. Booker T. Washington played
       in her husband's work. She taught school at the age of
       fourteen, acted in the capacity of "Mother Confessor" at
       Tuskegee Institute, began a plantation settlement 8 miles
       from Tuskegee and worked diligently with her husband in his
       efforts.

505   Scott, Hazel. "The Truth About Me." Ebony, (September 1960),
       pp. 137-144.
          Miss Scott comments on her controversial marriage, to
       Adam Clayton Powell, Jr., and also scores show business
       evils. She states that she does care about people and she
       has dedicated her life to helping other people, especially,
       alcholics and drug users.

506   Scott, Patricia Bell. "The English Language and Black Woman-
       hood: A Low Blow at Self-Esteem." The Journal of Afro-
       American Issues, 2 (Summer 1974), pp. 218-225.
          Contends that Black women have been victims of both rac-
       ism and sexism. The English language has dealt a "low
       blow" to the self-esteem of developing Black womanhood.
       Surmises that the impetus of the Blacks' fight against the
       racism and sexism of the English language as it relates to
       Black womanhood, must begin with Black women.

507   Seeber, Edward D. "Phillis Wheatley." Journal of Negro
       History, 24 (July 1939), pp. 259-262.
          An assessment of Phillis Wheatley and her poetry. Be-
       lieves that Miss Wheatley has not received sufficient recog-
       nition for her genius.

508   Shapiro, Samuel. "Black Women and the Blues: The Social
       Content of Bessie Smith's Music." Northwest Journal of
       African and Black American Studies, 2 (Winter 1974),
       pp. 11-19.
          Contends that Miss Smith's music had a social message for
       Black people. Concludes that within the limits imposed on
       Miss Smith who was born at an inauspicious time and place,
       she was proud of herself and her heritage and her people.

509   Shockley, Ann Allen. "The New Black Feminists." Northwest
Journal of African and Black American Studies, 2 (Winter
1974), pp. 1-5.
    Feels that the Black feminist promotes and reveals the
best of Black womanhood, her faith in herself, her family,
her children, and a belief in a better world. It is this
Black woman who is finding that to live totally, there must
be love of self and justice in this land.

510   _____. "The Negro Woman in Retrospect." Negro History
Bulletin, 29 (December 1965), pp. 55-56, 62, 70.
    Discusses the role Black women have played throughout
American History. Also mentions individual Black women.

511   _____. "Pauline Elizabeth Hopkins: Biographical Excursion
into Obscurity." Phylon, 33 (Spring 1972).
    Tells of one of the most neglected early Black women writ-
ers in America--Pauline Elizabeth Hopkins. Miss Hopkins
was born in 1859 in Portland, Maine and died on August 13,
1930 in Cambridge, Mass.

512   Silone-Yates, Josephine. "The National Association of
Colored Women." The Voice of the Negro, (July 1904),
pp. 283-287.
    Discusses the events surrounding the formation of the
National Association of Colored Women, which was founded in
Washington, D.C. in 1896.

513   Sissle, Nobel. "How Jo Baker Got Started." Negro Digest,
(August 1951), pp. 15-19.
    The story of Josephine Baker's rise to fame as told by
one of those who helped her when she first came to Broadway
at the age of 15.

514   Sizemore, Barbara A. "Sexism and the Black Male." Black
Scholar, 4 (March-April 1973), pp. 2-11.
    Includes a discussion on: (1) The myth of the Black
matriarchy, (2) a comparison of the status of Black women
with white women in terms of marriage or the accessibility
of males for marriages, education, income and political
participation, (3) an examination of the ideology of several Black men, and (4) an indication of some recommenda-
tions for the future. Concludes that Black women must
remember that the largest single group in support of male
superiority is women. Therefore, the fight must begin
there--with ourselves.

515   Slater, Jack. "Suicide: A Growing Menace to Black Women."
Ebony, (September 1973), pp. 152-160.
    During the past twenty years, the suicide rate of Black
American women has risen eighty percent. Reasons are given
for this drastic increase.

516 Slowe, Lucy D. "Higher Education for Negro Women." The
Journal of Negro Education, 2 (July 1933), pp. 352-358.
A historical overview of higher education for Black women
in the United States. Believes that education must fit
Black women for the highest development of their own gifts.

517 Smallwood, Bill. "The Girl with Golden Hands." The Brown
American, (December 1940), p. 7.
Mildred Blount, a young Black woman, designed hats for
movie studios, and movie stars in the 1940's.

518 Smith, Grace Ferguson. "Sojourner Truth--Listener to the
Voice." Negro History Bulletin, 36 (March 1973), pp. 63-65.
Tells of the first Black antislavery pilgrim, Sojourner
Truth, and how from the time she was a child, she talked and
listened to God. "Is God Dead?" are the words engraved on
her tombstone in Battle Creek, Michigan, where she died in
1883, having been a sojourner of this earth for nearly
eighty-six years.

519 Smith, Mary. "Birth Control and the Negro Woman." Ebony,
(March 1968), pp. 29-37.
The loudest protestors against birth control are Black
men, not Black women.

520 Smith, William G. "Ethel Waters." Phylon, 11 (Summer 1950),
pp. 114-120.
An assessment of the life and times of the great Black
actress and singer. Miss Waters was born October 31, 1900
and is still active today as a member of the Billy Graham
Crusades.

521 Southerland, Ellease. "Zora Neale Hurston: The Novelist-
Anthropologist's Life/Work." Black World, (August 1974),
pp. 20-30.
A biographical sketch and assessment of Mrs. Hurston's
life and publications over the years.

522 Staples, Mildred. "How I Got My Start." Opportunity, 26
(January-March 1948), pp. 16-17.
About a young Black woman who began as an interior deco-
rator in Peoria, Ohio.

523 Staples, Robert. "Mystique of Black Sexuality." Liberator,
7 (March 1967), pp. 8-10.
Discusses the historical views of Black sexuality. Feels
that most Whites believe that Black men, and especially
Black women, are sexually superior than white men and women.

524 _____. "The Myth of the Black Matriarchy." The Black
Scholar, (February 1970), pp. 8-16.

(_____.)
    In order to explore the myth of a Black female matriarchy,
one must understand the historical role of the Black woman
and the development of that role as it was influenced by the
political and economic organization of American Society.

525   _____. "The Myth of the Impotent Black Male." The Black
      Scholar, 2 (June 1971), pp. 2-9.
      Contends that the assault on Black masculinity is made
Precisely because Black males are men; not because they are
impotent. Dr. Staples concludes that while racists fanta-
size about the impotency of the Black man, his childlike
status, the liberation struggle will proceed, with one
uncompromising goal: total freedom for all Black people,
men and women alike.

526   Stokes, Gail. "Black Woman to Black Man." Liberator, 8
      (December 1968), p. 17.
      A Black woman discusses briefly how Black women have been
treated over the years and concludes that the Black man must
give Black women respect due them.

527   "Stress and Strains on Black Women." Ebony, (June 1974),
      pp. 33-40.
      Tells how Black women's mental and physical health has
become a most critical issue. Some of their stress has
been caused by hypertension, depression, cancer, suicide,
and sterilization.

528   Stone, Louise D. "What It's Like to be a Colored Woman."
      Washington Post, (13 November 1966), p. 43.
      A narrative discussing the positive and negative attri-
butes of the Black woman, and the social and psychological
impediments that she must face.

529   Strong, Augusta. "Negro Women in Freedom's History Battles."
      Freedomways, (Fall 1967), pp. 302-315.
      An assessment of a number of Black women and the role they
played in Black people's stride for freedom.

530   Terrell, Mary Church. "Lynching from a Negro's Point of
      View." North American Review, 178 (July 1904), pp. 853-898.
      Mary Church Terrell, honorary president of the National
Association of Colored Women, discusses the phenomena of
lynching from the Black man's viewpoint. Some discussion of
the Klu Klux Klan as a form of organized violence is also
mentioned.

531   _____. "The Progress of Colored Women." The Voice of the
      Negro, (July 1904), pp. 291-294.
      Discusses the social, political, business, and economical
advancement of Black women over the years. Surmises that in

(Terrell, Mary Church)
a variety of ways Black women are rendering valiant service
to their race.

532 "The Negro Woman Goes to Market." The Brown American, 1-3
(April 1936), p. 13.
About the buying power of "Mrs. Brown America," and how
she should buy from Black-owned establishments.

533 Thompson, Era Bell. "Love Comes to Mahalia Jackson." Ebony,
(November 1964), pp. 50-60.
Discusses Miss Jackson's personal life and tells how she
has added a housewife's role to her musical career since she
got married.

534 Thorpe, Claiburne B. "Aspiration: An Index of Black Female
Personality." Journal of Social and Behavioral Sciences, 20
(Summer-Fall 1972), pp. 8-12.
Discusses Blacks in general; however, mentions briefly the
relationship of the Black child to his/her mother.

535 Tillman, Katherine D. "Paying Professions for Colored Girls."
The Voice of the Negro, (January and February 1907).
The professions discussed include teaching, nursing, mil-
linery, dress-making, hair-dressing, domestic science,
catering, etc.

536 Uggams, Leslie. "Why I Married an Australian." Ebony, (May
1967), pp. 140-141.
This famous singer-actress discusses her marriage to a
white man from Australia. Miss Uggams admits that both she
and her husband realized that their interracial marriage
would not be easy.

537 "Una Mae Carlisle." Ebony, (January 1952), pp. 51-53.
About a Black popular singer who is the only Black musician with her own coast-to-coast network radio program.

538 Valien, Preston. "Attitudes of the Negro Mother toward Birth
Control." American Journal of Sociology, 55 (1949),
pp. 279-283.
Of the 136 southern urban Negro mothers interviewed,
approximately one-half had unfavorable attitudes toward
birth control practices. Due to religious or moral reasons
they believed that birth control was inefficient or injurious
to their health. Age, number of children, urban or rural
birthplace, and amount of education appear to be associated
with differential attitudes toward birth control.

539 Veasey, Jess F. "Black Youth's Reading Skills and Achievement
as a Function of Single Parent Household with Mothers as
Head vs. Both Parents being Present." The Journal of

(Veasey, Jess F.)
Afro-American Issues, 2 (Summer 1974), pp. 267-280.
Concludes that the learning ability of children from disadvantaged homes may be due to environmental factors as much
as from the fact that they come from mother-headed house-
holds.

540 Walworth, D. "My Most Unforgettable Character: Mary McLeod
Bethune." Reader's Digest, (February 1952), pp. 146-151.
A short biography of Mary McLeod Bethune. It points out
the contributions she made in the area of education. Mrs.
Bethune established several schools for Black women.

541 Washington, Mary Helen. "Black Women Image Makers." Black
World, (August 1974), pp. 10-19.
Discusses the many negative presentations and false depic-
tions of Black women seen in the media and in literature.
Tells of some Black women writers who are trying to change
the stereotypes through their writings.

542 Washington, Mrs. Booker T. "Social Improvement of the Plantation Woman." The Voice of the Negro, (July 1904),
pp. 288-290.
Concludes that the plantation Black woman will not prove
to be a "menace" to her race, but will instead be a deliv-
erer. Through the Black woman will come the earnest, faithful service for the highest development of home and family.
that will result in the solution of the so-called race
problem.

543 Waters, Ethel. "The Men in My Life." Ebony, (January 1952),
pp. 24-33.
Famous actress-singer looks back to recall intimate off-
stage story of the tumultuous loves in her stormy life on
stage.

544 Watkins, Francess Ellen. "Our Great Want." The Anglo-
African Magazine, 1 (1859), p. 160.
Miss Watkins, a leading Black woman writer in the 1800s
states that the greatest need of Black people is not gold or
silver, talent or genius, but true men and women. She concludes that we need men and women devoted to the cause of
emancipation and universal freedom.

545 Watson, Florence Peters. "A Negro Woman Looks at War." The
Brown American, (May 1941), p. 21.
Mrs. Watson points out that Black women in the United
States are ready and willing to assist the War efforts.

546 Watson, Vernaline. "Self-Concept Formation and the Afro-
American Women." The Journal of Afro-American Issues, 2
(Summer 1974), pp. 226-236.

(Watson, Vernaline)

Contends that Black American women have used, and continue to use, a variety of techniques for self-development. Prof. Watson believes that it is possible for one to exist in a difficult and oppressive environment without developing self-attitudes of hatred and rejection.

547   Westoff, Charles F. and Ryder, Norman B. "Contraceptive Practice Among Urban Blacks in the United States, 1965." The Milbank Memorial Fund Quarterly, 43 (April 1970), pp. 215-239.

A report on the practice of contraception and family planning among the urban Black population of the United States, with special emphasis on their use of newer methods. Concludes that urban Black women are more informed about the use of contraceptives than are Black women in suburban or rural areas.

548   Whiting, Helen Adele. "Slave Adventures: Harriet and Her Caravans." Negro History Bulletin, 19 (April 1956), p. 164.

A short, one page, article on the many ways Harriet Tubman helped slaves escape from the South to freedom in the North, and Canada.

549   Williams, Bertha M. "Black Women: Assertive vs. Aggressiveness." The Journal of Afro-American Issues, 2 (Summer 1974), pp. 204-211.

About the exploration of the Black woman's potential for growth, the concept of effective interpersonal relationships, and self-enhancement through self-assertiveness. Concludes that the Black woman must destroy the myth and make it clear that she is important and so are others, not only because others imply or suggest it, but because she herself knows it.

550   Williams, Rev. Cecil. "A Conversation with Angela." Black Scholar, 3 (March-April 1973), pp. 36-48.

An exclusive interview with Angela Davis while she was on trial on charges of murder, kidnap and conspiracy to commit both. A variety of topics are discussed and there are several photos of Miss Davis and some of her supporters.

551   Williams, Daniel H. "Ovarian Cysts in Colored Women." Philadelphia Medical Journal, (29 December 1900).

Refutes the idea that Black women do not have ovarian tumors. The record of the cases collected by Dr. Williams, a Black surgeon, furnished sufficient data to sustain his contention.

552   Williams, Emily H. "The National Association of Colored Women." Southern Workman, 43 (December 1914), pp. 564-566.

Discusses the status and general improvement of Black women in Chicago in terms of improvement in home life,

(Williams, Emily H.)
employment as teachers, domestics and industrial labor, and
the establishment of the Phyllis Wheatley Home.

553   Williams, Fannie Barrier. "The Club Movement Among Colored
Women." The Voice of the Negro, (March 1904), pp. 99-102.
Discusses the Club movement among Black women and concludes that it is still vital for Black women of America to
organize and remain organized for practical usefulness in
the social uplift of the Negro (Black) race.

554   _____. "The Colored Girl." The Voice of the Negro, (June
1905), pp. 400-403.
The way to exalt the Black girl is to place a higher pre-
mium on character than we do upon the quality of her occupa-
tion. A fine girl is the supreme thing. Let the Black
girl be loved, admired, encouraged, and above all things
heroically protected against the scorn and contempt of men,
Black as well as white.

·555   Williams, Sylvanie Fancaz. "The Social Status of the Negro
Woman." The Voice of the Negro, (July 1904), pp. 298-300.
In order to judge the Black woman one must see her in her
home, for there one will find her loyal and diligent in her
womanhood, strong and brave in her faith, and it is there
where she is displaying powers of endurance in times of
trial and sorrow.

556   Wisham, Betty. "Yvonne Brathwaite Burke: Day by Day."
Essence, (November 1974), p. 73.
A political-biographical sketch of the Congresswoman from
California is given. Tells of Yvonne Burkes day by day work
to wield the laws to feed the hungry children, to provide
jobs for the needy, to bring equality to people regardless
of their sex, color, and creed.

557   Winslow, T. S. "Treasure: Life of a Colored Maid." American
Mercury, (February 1933), pp. 149-152.
A descriptive essay about the author's Black maid named
Edna. Presents a typical white mentality toward Blacks.

558   "Women at War." The Brown American, (Summer 1943), p. 3.
Discusses the Black woman's contributions to the war
efforts.

559   "Women....In Civic Affairs and in the Creative Arts." Opportunity, 24 (October-December 1948), pp. 138-140.
A discussion of Black women in civic affairs in Fort
Worth, Texas, and in Cleveland, Ohio. There are photos of
two of these women in this article.

560   "Women in Uniform." Ebony, (December 1962), pp. 62-67.
      Tells of the many jobs open to Black women in uniform and
      how they have shared in the significant, supportive role as
      women members of the Army, Navy, and later the Marines,
      Coast Guard, and Air Force.

561   Woodson, Carter G. "Emma Frances Grayson Merritt." Opportu-
      nity, 8 (August 1930), pp. 244-245.
      Miss Merritt was a Black woman born January 11, 1860 in
      Dumfries, Virginia, who later became a leading educator.
      Among her major achievements include the organization and
      presidency of the Teacher's Benefit and Annuity Assocation
      and the Prudence Crandall Association.

562   Wright, Sarah E. "The Negro Woman in American Literature."
      Freedomways, 6 (Winter 1966), pp. 8-25.
      Black women have been omitted as important subject matter
      in the media. However, a number of Black women are pres-
      ently expressing themselves in various ways through the
      media.

GENERAL REFERENCE WORKS

563   Brignano, Russell C. Black Americans in Autobiography. Duke
       University Press, Durham, N. C., 1974.

563a   Dannett, Sylvia G. L. Profiles of Negro Womanhood. M. W.
       Lads, New York, 1964.

564   Davis, John P. (ed), The American Negro Reference Book.
       Prentice-Hall, Englewood Cliffs, N. J., 1966.

565   Davis, Lenwood G. Blacks in the Cities, 1900-1975. Council
       of Planning Librarians, Monticello, Illinois, 1975.

566   _____. The Black Family in Urban Areas in the United States.
       Council of Planning Librarians, Monticello, Illinois, 1975.

567   _____. Black Women in the Cities. Council of Planning
       Librarians, Monticello, Illinois, 1975.

568   Finney, James E. The Long Road to Now: A Bibliography of
       Material Relating to the American Black Man. Charles W.
       Clark Co., New York, 1969.

569   Fleming, G. James and Burkel, Christian E. Who's Who in
       Colored America. Christian E. Burkel and Associates,
       Yonkers-on-Hudson, New York, 1950.

570   Gloster, Hugh. Negro Voices in American Fiction. University
       of North Carolina Press, Chapel Hill, 1948.

571   Green, Elizabeth L. The Negro in Contemporary American
       Literature. University of North Carolina Press, Chapel
       Hill, 1928.

572   Homer, Dorothy R. The Negro in the United States: A List of
       Significant Books, New York Public Library, New York, 1965.

573   Indiana University. The Black Family and the Black Woman: A
       Bibliography. Indiana University Library and the Afro-
       American Studies Dept., Bloomington, Indiana, 1972.

574   Katz, William Loren. Teachers' Guide to American Negro
      History. Quadrangle Books, Chicago, 1968.

575   Lewinson, Paul. A Guide to Documents in the National Archives
      for Negro Studies. American Council of Learned Societies,
      Washington, 1947.

576   Mather, Frank Lincoln. Who's Who of the Colored Race: A
      General Bibliographical Dictionary of Men and Women of
      African Descent. Vol. 1. N. P., Chicago, 1915.

577   Miller, Elizabeth W. The Negro in the United States: A
      Bibliography. Harvard University Press, Cambridge, Mass.,
      1966.

578   Ploski, Harry A. Reference Library of Black America.
      Bellwether Publishing Co., New York, 1971, 3 Vols.

579   Porter, Dorothy B. A Working Bibliography on the Negro in the
      United States. University Microfilms, Ann Arbor, Michigan,
      1969.

580   _____. The Negro in the United States. The Library of
      Congress, Washington, 1970.

581   Salk, Erwin A. A Layman's Guide to Negro History. McGraw-
      Hill, New York, 1967.

582   Schatz, Walter. Directory of Afro-American Resources.
      R. R. Bowker Co., New York, 1970.

583   Shockley, Ann Allen and Chandler, Sue P. Living Black
      American Authors: A Biographical Directory. R. R.
      Bowker Co., New York, 1973.

584   Smith, Dwight L. Afro-American History: A Bibliography.
      ABC-CLIO, Inc., Santa Barbara, 1974.

585   Sprangler, Earl. Bibliography of Negro History. Ross and
      Haines, Minneapolis, 1963.

586   Thompson, Edgar T. and Thompson, Alma. Race and Region: A
      Descriptive Bibliography Compiled with Special Reference to
      Relations between Whites and Negroes in the United States.
      University of North Carolina Press, Chapel Hill, 1949.

587   Turner, Lorenzo C. Anti-Slavery Sentiment in American Litera-
      ture Prior to 1865. Kennikat Press, Port Washington, New
      York, 1966.

588   Welsch, Erwin K. The Negro in the United States: A Research
      Guide. Indiana University Press, Bloomington, 1965.

589   Whiteman, Maxwell. A Century of Fiction by American Negroes
      1853-1952: A Descriptive Bibliography. M. Jacobs,
      Philadelphia, 1955.

590   Williams, Ora. American Black Women in the Arts and Social
      Sciences: A Bibliographic Survey. Scarecrow Press,
      Metuchen, N. J., 1973.

591   Work, Monroe N. A Bibliography of the Negro in Africa and
      America. Octagon Books, Inc., New York, 1966.

592. SELECTED CURRENT BLACK PERIODICALS: DIRECTORY

BLACK ACADEMY REVIEW. 3296 Main St., Buffalo, New York, 14214. Quarterly. 1970 -

BLACK DIALOGUE. Box 1019, New York, 10027. Quarterly. 1970 -

BLACK ENTERPRISE. 295 Madison Avenue, New York, 10017. Monthly. 1970 -

BLACK POLITICIAN. 955 South Western Avenue, Suite 210, Los Angeles, California, 90006. Quarterly. 1969 -

BLACK SCHOLAR. Box 908, Sausalito, California, 94965. Monthly except July and August. 1969 -

BLACK WORLD. (Formerly NEGRO DIGEST). Johnson Publishing Company, 1820 South Michigan Avenue, Chicago, Illinois, 60616. Monthly. 1942 -

CLA JOURNAL. Official Publication of the College Language Association, Morgan State College, Baltimore, Maryland. Monthly. 1942 -

CRISIS. Organ of the National Association for the Advancement of Colored People. The Crisis Publishing Company, Inc. 1790 Broadway, New York, New York, 10019. Monthly from October to May and Bi-Monthly June-July, August-September. 1910 -

EBONY. Johnson Publishing Company, 1820 South Michigan Avenue, Chicago, Illinois, 60616. Monthly. 1945 -

ENCORE. 572 Madison Avenue, New York, New York, 10022. Monthly. 1972 -

ESSENCE: The Magazine for Today's Black Woman. 300 E. 42nd Street, New York, 10016. Monthly. 1970 -

FREEDOMWAYS: A Quarterly Review of the Negro Freedom
Movement. Freedomway Associates, 799 Broadway, New York,
New York, 10013. Quarterly. 1961 -

JET. Johnson Publishing Company, 1820 South Michigan Avenue,
Chicago, Illinois, 60616. Weekly. 1951 -

JOURNAL OF AFRO-AMERICAN ISSUES. 1629 K Street, N. W.,
Suite 520, Washington, D.C., 20006. Weekly. 1951 -

JOURNAL OF BLACK STUDIES. 275 South Beverlyn Drive, Beverly
Hills, California, 90212. Quarterly, 1970 -

JOURNAL OF HUMAN RELATIONS. Central State College,
Wilberforce, Ohio, 45384. Quarterly. 1952 -

JOURNAL OF NEGRO EDUCATION. Published for the Bureau of
Education Research by Howard University Press, Washington,
D.C., 20001. Quarterly. 1932 -

JOURNAL OF NEGRO HISTORY. The Association for the Study of
Afro-American Life and History, Inc., 1538 Ninth Street,
N. W., Washington, D.C., 20001. Quarterly. 1916 -

LIBERATOR. Afro-American Research Institute, Inc., 244 East
Street, New York, New York, 10017. Monthly. 1961 -

MUHAMMAD SPEAKS. Published by Muhammad's Mosque No. 2, 2548
South Federal Street, Chicago, Illinois, 60616. Weekly.
1960 -

NEGRO HERITAGE. 11372 Links Dr., Reston, Virginia, 22090.
Monthly. 1961 -

NEGRO HISTORY BULLETIN. The Association for the Study of
Afro-American Life and History, Inc., 1538 Ninth Street,
N. W., Washington, D.C., 20001. Monthly except June, July,
August and September. 1937 -

NEW SOUTH. Southern Regional Council, 5 Forsyth Street,
N. W., Atlanta 3, Georgia. Quarterly. 1946 -

OPPORTUNITY: JOURNAL OF NEGRO LIFE. National Urban League,
127 East 23rd Street, New York, New York, Vols. 1-17, 1923-
1943.

PHYLON. Atlanta University, Atlanta, Georgia. Quarterly.
1940 -

QUARTERLY REVIEW OF HIGHER EDUCATION AMONG NEGROES. Johnson
C. Smith University, Charlotte, North Carolina. Quarterly.
1933 -

RACE RELATIONS LAW REPORTER. Vanderbilt University School of
  Law, 131 21st Avenue, South, Nashville, Tennessee, 37203.
  Quarterly. 1956-1967.

RIGHTS AND REVIEWS, A Magazine of the Black Power Movement in
  America. New York Chapter of CORE, 200 West 135th Street,
  New York, New York, 10030. Irregular. 1964 -

SOULBOOK: The Quarterly Journal of Revolutionary Afro-
  America. Berkeley, California, P. O. Box 1097. Quarterly.

SEPIA. Sepia Publishing Company, 1220 Harding Street, Fort
  Worth, Texas, 76102. Monthly. 1959 -

REPORTS, PAMPHLETS, SPEECHES
AND
GOVERNMENT DOCUMENTS*

593   American Law and the Black Community viewed by Black Women
       Lawyers, Afro-American Studies Program. Boston University,
       Occasional paper, Number 1, 1974.

594   Bell, Alan P. Black Sexuality: Fact and Fancy. A paper
       presented to "Focus: Black America Series." Indiana
       University, October 1968.

595   Bell, Robert. "The One Parent Mother in the Negro Lower
       Class." Unpublished paper, presented to the Eastern
       Sociological Society, April 1965.

596   Coleman, James S. Equality of Educational Opportunity.
       Washington, D.C.: U.S. Department of Health, Education and
       Welfare. Document OE-38001, 1966.

597   Curtis, Rep. Thomas B. Supplementary View, in the U.S. Con-
       gress, Senate Joint Economic Committee, Report: Employment
       and Manpower Problems in the Cities--Implication of the
       Report of the National Advisory Commission on Civil Dis-
       orders, 90th Congress, 2nd Session, Report No. 1568.
       Washington, D.C.: U.S. Government Printing Office,
       16 September 1968.

598   Dodson, Jacqueline. "To Define Black Womanhood," Atlanta,
       Georgia: Institute of the Black World, February 1971.

599   Douglas, Joseph H. The Negro Family's Search for Economic
       Security. Washington, D.C.: U.S. Department of Health,
       Education and Welfare, July 1956.

600   DuBois, W. E. B., ed. Mortality Among Negroes in Cities,
       Together with Proceedings of the 1st Conference for the

*These materials include citations relevant to the Black Woman.

(DuBois, W. E. B., ed.)
Study of Negro Problems. Atlanta: Atlanta University
Press, 1899.

601 Emlen, John T. Report for the National Conference on Migra-
tion. National Urban League Papers, Library of Congress,
January 1917.

602 Evans, William. Race Fear and Housing. National Urban
League, 1946.

603 Federal Public Housing Authority. Experience in Public
Housing. Projects Jointly Occupied by Negro, White and
Other Tenants, 1944.

604 _____. Public Housing Available for Negroes, As of July 31,
1945. Report S-602, Statistics Division, 9 November 1945.

605 _____. Public Housing Available to Negroes, As of October 13,
1945. Report S-602, Statistics Division, 18 April 1946.

606 _____. Public Housing Available to Negroes, As of August 31,
1946. Report S-602, Statistics Division, 22 January 1947.

607 Fisher, Lloyd and Weckler, Joseph. The Problem of Violence.
American Council on Race Relations, 1946.

608 Gallagher, Ursula M. "Adoption, Current Trends, "Welfare
in Review. Washington, D.C.: U.S. Department of Health,
Education and Welfare, 5 February 1967.

609 Garrett, Beatrice L. "Meeting the Crisis in Foster Family
Care," Children. Department of Health, Education and
Welfare. Washington, D.C.: U.S. Government Printing
Office, 1966, 3-8.

610 Governor's Interracial Commission. The Negro and Home in
Minnesota. Minneapolis: The Commission, June 1947.

611 Herzog, Elizabeth, et al. Families for Black Children: The
Search for Adoptive Parents. A report of the Division of
Research and Evaluation, Children's Bureau, Office of Child
Development and the Social Research Group. Washington,
D.C.: The George Washington University, 1971.

612 Herzog, Elizabeth and Bernstein, Rose. "Why So Few Negro
Adoptions?" Children. U.S. Department of Health, Education
and Welfare, January-February 1965.

613 _____. Boys in Fatherless Families. U.S. Department of
Health, Education and Welfare. Washington, D.C.: Office of
Child Development, Children's Bureau, 1970.

614   Hewes, Laurence I., Jr. and Bell, William Y. Jr. Intergroup
       Relations in San Diego. American Council on Race Relations,
       1946.

615   Johnson, Charles S. and Associates. The Negro War Worker in
       San Francisco. San Francisco: San Francisco YWCA and
       others, 1944.

616   Keyserling, Mary Dublin. "The Negro Woman in the United
       States--New Roles--New Challenges." Speech before the
       National Association of Colored Women's Clubs Convention,
       Oklahoma City, Oklahoma, 27 July 1966.

617   _____. "Women, Work and Poverty." Speech before Conference
       of Women in the War on Poverty, Washington, D.C.,
       8 May 1967.

618   Lampman, Robert. "The Low Income Population and Economic
       Growth." Study Paper No. 12. Washington, D.C.: United
       States Congress Joint Economic Committee, 1959.

619   Lawder, Elizabeth A. "Quasi-Adoption." Meeting the Crisis
       in Foster Family Care. U.S. Department of Health, Educa-
       tion and Welfare. Washington, D.C.: U.S. Government
       Printing Office, 1966.

620   Manpower Report of the President. Superintendent of Docu-
       ments. Washington, D.C., March 1965.

621   Martz, Helen E. "Illegitimacy and Dependency," Indicators,
       U.S. Department of Health, Education and Welfare, reprint
       September 1963.

622   Matthews, V. C. "Dangers Encountered by Southern Girls in
       Northern Cities." Hampton Negro Conference, Proceedings,
       July 1898.

623   Moynihan, Daniel P. The Negro Family: The Case for National
       Action. Washington, D.C.: U.S. Department of Labor,
       Office of Planning and Research, 1965.

624   Murray, Pauli. "The Negro Woman in the Quest for Equality."
       Paper presented at Leadership Conference, National Council
       of Negro Women, Washington, D.C. November 1963.

625   National Association for the Advancement of Colored People.
       Memorandum Concerning Present Discriminatory Practices of
       Federal Housing Administration, 26 October 1944.

626   National Association of Social Workers and Washington Center
       for Metropolitan Studies. The Public Welfare Crisis in the

(National Association of Social Workers...)
Nation's Capital, A Call to the Conscience of the Community,
Washington, D.C., 1963.

627 National Catholic Welfare Conference. Seminar on Negro Problems in the Field of Social Action, 1946.

627a National Urban League Report. Performance of Negro Workers
in 300 War Plants, New York: National Urban League,
1 February 1944.

628 Negro Status and Race Relations in the United States, 1911-
1946. The Thirty-Five Year Report of the Phelps-Stokes
Fund, New York, 1946.

629 Report of the National Advisory Commission on Civil Disorders,
Washington, D.C.: U.S. Government Printing Office, 1968.

630 Report of the President's Commission on the Status of Women.
American Women, Washington, D.C.: Superintendent of
Documents, 1963.

631 Stone, Robert C. and Schlamp, F. T. "Family Life Styles
below the Poverty Line: A Report to the State Social Welfare Board for the Institute for Social Science Research,"
San Francisco State College, 1966.

632 To Establish Justice, To Insure Domestic Tranquility: Final
Report of the National Commission on the Causes and Preven-
tion of Violence, Washington, D.C.: Government Printing
Office, December 1969.

633 United States Bureau of the Census. "Trends in Social and
Economic Conditions of Negroes in the United States,"
Washington, D.C.: U.S. Government Printing Office, Current
Population Report, No. 27, 7 February 1969, p. 23.

633a _____. "Recent Trends in Social and Economic Conditions of
Negroes in the United States," Washington, D.C.: U.S.
Government Printing Office, 1968.

634 _____. "Measuring the Quality of Housing: An Appraisal of
the Census Statistics and Methods," Washington, D.C.: U.S.
Government Printing Office, 1967 (a).

635 _____. "Poverty Areas in the 100 Largest Metropolitan Areas,
1960 census of population, supplementary reports PC(SI)-54,"
Washington, D.C.: U.S. Government Printing Office,
13 November 1967.

636 _____. "Social and Economic Conditions of Negroes in the
United States," Washington, D.C.: U.S. Government Printing
Office, 1967 (b).

637   _____. "Selected Characteristics of Persons and Families, March 1970," Current Population Reports, Population Charac-teristics, Series P-20, No. 204, 13 July 1970.

638   _____. "Probabilities of Marriage, Divorce and Remarriage," Current Population Reports, Special Studies, Series P-23, No. 32, 29 July 1970.

639   _____. "Educational Attainment: March 1970," Current Popula-tion Reports, Population Characteristics, Series P-20, No. 207, 30 November 1970, Table 1.

640   _____. "Income in 1969 of Families and Persons in the United States," Current Population Reports, Consumer Income, Series P-60, No. 75, 14 December 1970.

641   _____. "Differences Between Income of White and Negro Husband-Wife Families are Relatively Small Outside the South," U.S. Department of Commerce News, 19 February 1971.

642   _____. "Fertility Indicators: 1970," Current Population Reports, Special Studies, Series P-23, No. 36, 16 April 1971.

643   _____. "Median Family Income up in 1970," Current Population Reports, Consumer Income, Series P-60, No. 78, 20 May 1971.

644   _____. "Poverty Increases by 1.2 Million in 1970," Current Population Reports, Consumer Income, Series P-60, No. 77, 7 May 1971.

645   _____. "The Social and Economic Status of Negroes in the United States, 1970," Current Population Reports, Special Studies, Series P-23, No. 38, and BLS Report, No. 394.

646   United States Commission on Civil Rights. Racism in America and How to Combat It, Clearing House Publication, Urban Series No. 1, Washington, D.C.: Government Printing Office, January 1970.

647   United States Department of Commerce and Labor. Conditions of Living Among the Poor, Bureau of Labor Bulletin 64, Washington, D.C.: U.S. Government Printing Office, 1966.

648   United States Department of Health, Education and Welfare, Social Security Administration, "The Aged Negro and His Income," Social Security Bulletin, February 1964.

649   _____. "The Poor--Some Facts and Some Fictions," Bureau Pub-lication No. 451, Washington, D.C.: U.S. Government Print-ing Office, 1967.

650   United States Department of Health, Education and Welfare,
      Social Security Administration. "Who's Who Among the Poor:
      A Demographic View of Poverty," Social Security Bulletin,
      July 1965.

651   _____. Children's Bureau, "Child Labor and the Work of Moth-
      ers in Oyster and Shrimp Canning Communities on the Gulf
      Coast," by Viola I. Paradise, Bureau Publication No. 98,
      Washington, D.C.: U.S. Government Printing Office, 1922.

652   _____. "Child Labor and the Work of Mothers on Norfolk Truck
      Farms," Bureau publication No. 130, Washington D.C.: U.S.
      Government Printing Office, 1924.

653   _____. "Child Labor on Maryland Truck Farms," by Alice
      Channing, Bureau Publication No. 123. Washington, D.C.:
      U.S. Government Printing Office, 1923.

654   _____. "Children of the Poor," Social Security Bulletin,
      Washington, D.C.: U.S. Government Printing Office, July
      1963.

655   _____. "Counting the Poor: Another Look at the Poverty
      Profile," Social Security Bulletin, Washington, D.C.:
      U.S. Government Printing Office, January 1965.

656   _____. "Welfare of Children in Cotton-growing areas of
      Texas," Bureau of Publications No. 134, Washington, D.C.:
      U.S. Government Printing Office, 1924.

657   _____. America's Children and Youth in Institutions, 1950-
      1960-1964, Children's Bureau, 1964.

658   _____. Vital Statistics of the U.S., 1968, Vol 1-Natality,
      National Center for Health Statistics, 1968.

659   _____. Adoptions in 1969; Supplement to Child Welfare Sta-
      tistics--1969, National Center for Social Statistics, 1969.

660   _____. "Preliminary Report on Findings--1969 AFDC Study,"
      National Center for Social Statistics, Social and Rehabili-
      tation Service, March 1970.

660a United States Department of Housing and Urban Development.
      "In-Cities Experimental Housing Research and Development
      Project," Phase I Composite Report, User Needs, March 1969.

661   _____. "Problems of the Negro in the City," address by Walter
      B. Lewis, Washington, D.C.: U.S. Government Printing
      Office, 20 April 1968.

662   United States Department of Labor.   "A Sharper Look at Unem-
      ployment in United States Cities and Slums," 1967.

663   _____. "Labor Force Projection by Color, 1970-80," Special
      Labor Force Report No. 73, Washington, D.C.:   U.S. Govern-
      ment Printing Office.

664   _____. "Black Americans: A Decade of Occupational Changes,"
      Publication No. 1731, Washington, D.C.:   U.S. Government
      Printing Office, 1972.

665   _____. Manpower Report of the President, 1970, Washington,
      D.C.:   U.S. Government Printing Office, April 1968.

666   _____. "Negro Employment in the South, Volume I: The
      Houston Labor Market," Manpower Research Monograph No. 23,
      Washington, D.C.:   U.S. Government Printing Office, 1971.

667   _____. Negroes in the United States: Their Economic and
      Social Situation, Bulletin No. 1511, Washington, D.C.:
      U.S. Government Printing Office, 1966.

668   United States Department of Labor and Department of Commerce.
      "The Social and Economic Status of Negroes in the United
      States," Washington, D.C.:   U.S. Government Printing Office,
      1969.

669   United States Department of Labor, Women's Bureau. "Domestic
      Workers and Their Employment Relations. A Study Based on
      the Records of the Domestic Efficiency Association of
      Baltimore, Maryland," Bulletin No. 12, Washington, D.C.:
      U.S. Government Printing Office, 1924.

670   _____. "Women in Alabama Industries," Bureau Bulletin No. 34,
      Washington, D.C.:   U.S. Government Printing Office, 1924.

671   _____. "Women in Arkansas Industries. A Study of Hours,
      Wages, and Working Conditions," Bureau Bulletin No. 26,
      Washington, D.C.:   U.S. Government Printing Office, 1923.

672   _____. "Women in Delaware Industries. A Study of Hours,
      Wages and Working Conditions," Bureau Bulletin No. 58,
      Washington, D.C.:   U.S. Government Printing Office, 1927.

673   _____. "Women in Georgia Industries," Bureau Bulletin No. 22,
      Washington, D.C.:   U.S. Government Printing Office, 1922.

674   _____. "Women in Illinois Industries. A Study of Hours, and
      Working Conditions," Bureau Bulletin No. 51, Washington,
      D.C.:   U.S. Government Printing Office. 1926.

675   United States Department of Labor, Women's Bureau. "Women in
       Kentucky Industries. A Study of Hours, Wages, and Working
       Conditions," Bureau Bulletin No. 29, Washington, D.C.:
       U.S. Government Printing Office, 1923.

676   _____. "Women in Maryland Industries," Bureau Bulletin No.
       24, Washington, D.C.: U.S. Government Printing Office,
       1923.

677   _____. "Women in Mississippi Industries. A Study of Hours,
       Wages, and Working Conditions," Bureau Bulletin No. 55,
       Washington, D.C.: U.S. Government Printing Office, 1926.

678   _____. "Women in Missouri Industries," Bureau Bulletin No.
       35, Washington, D.C.: U.S. Government Printing Office, 1924.

679   _____. "Women in New Jersey Industries. A Study of Wages and
       Hours," Bureau Bulletin No. 37, Washington, D.C.: U.S.
       Government Printing Office, 1924.

680   _____. "Women in Ohio Industries. A Study of Hours, Wages,
       and Working Conditions," Bureau Bulletin No. 44, Washington,
       D.C.: U.S. Government Printing Office, 1925.

681   _____. "Women in Oklahoma Industries. A Study of Hours,
       Wages, and Working Conditions," Bureau Bulletin No. 48,
       Washington, D.C.: U.S. Government Printing Office, 1926.

682   _____. "Women in Poverty--Jobs and the Need for Jobs,"
       Washington, D.C.: U.S. Government Printing Office, April
       1968.

683   _____. "Women in South Carolina Industries. A Study of
       Hours, Wages, and Working Conditions," Bureau Bulletin No.
       32, Washington, D.C.: U.S. Government Printing Office,
       1923.

684   _____. "Women in Tennessee Industries. A Study of Hours,
       Wages, and Working Conditions," Washington, D.C.: U.S.
       Government Printing Office, 1927.

685   _____. "Women in the Labor Force," Washington, D.C.: U.S.
       Government Printing Office, January 1972.

686   _____. "Women Workers in Regional Areas and in Large States
       and Metropolitan Areas," Washington, D.C.: U.S. Government
       Printing Office, March 1972.

687   _____. "Educational Attainment of Nonwhite Women,"
       Washington, D.C.: U.S. Government Printing Office, August
       1968.

688   _____. "Growing up Poor: An Overview and Analysis of Child-rearing and Family Life Patterns Associated with Poverty," Bureau Publication, Washington, D.C.: U.S. Government Printing Office, 13 May 1966.

689   _____. "Guide to Sources of Data on Women and Women Workers for the United States and for Regions, States and Local Areas," Washington, D.C.: U.S. Government Printing Office, March 1972.

690   _____. "Hours and Conditions of Work for Women in Industry in Virginia," Bureau Bulletin No. 10, Washington, D.C.: U.S. Government Printing Office, 1920.

691   _____. "Negro Women in Industry in 15 States," Washington, D.C.: U.S. Government Printing Office, 1929.

692   _____. "Nonwhite Women Workers," Washington, D.C.: U.S. Government Printing Office, October 1966.

693   _____. "Negro Women Workers in 1960," Bureau Publication No. 287, Washington, D.C.: U.S. Government Printing Office, 1963.

694   _____. "Negro Women in the Population and in the Labor Force," Washington, D.C.: U.S. Government Printing Office, December 1967.

695   _____. "The New Position of Women in American Industry," Bureau Bulletin No. 12, Washington, D.C.: U.S. Government Printing Office, 1920.

696   _____. "The Occupational Progress of Women. An Interpretation of Census Statistics of Women in Gainful Occupations," Bureau Bulletin No. 27, Washington, D.C.: U.S. Government Printing Office, 1922.

697   _____. "This We Have Done: A Report in Progress, July 1, 1970-June 30, 1971," Washington, D.C.: U.S. Government Printing Office, 1971.

698   _____. "Women's Earnings in Poor Families," Washington, D.C.: U.S. Government Printing Office, January 1967.

699   _____. "Women's Employment in Vegetable Canneries in Delaware," Bureau Bulletin No. 62, Washington, D.C.: U.S. Government Printing Office, 1927.

700   United States Manpower Administration. "Civil Rights in the Urban Crisis," by Donald Slaiman, Washington, D.C.: U.S. Government Printing Office, 1968.

701   United States National Commission on Urban Problems.   "The
      Large Poor Family--a Housing Gap," by Walter Smart and oth-
      ers, Research Report No. 4, Washington, D.C.:   U.S. Govern-
      ment Printing Office, 1968.

UNITED STATES LIBRARIES
WITH
MAJOR BLACK HISTORY COLLECTIONS

702   Bennett College, Thomas F. Holgate Library, Greensboro, N. C.
      (Excellent collections on Black women).

703   Bronxville Public Library, 201 Pondfield, Bronxville, N. Y.
      Books presented in honor of Dr. Ralph J. Bunche, for books
      by and of Blacks.

704   Columbia University Libraries, Special Collections, Alexander
      Gumby Collections, New York.

705   Detroit Public Library, Azalia Hackley Music Library, 5201
      Woodward, Detroit, Michigan.

706   Dillard University Library, 2601 Gentilly Blvd., New Orleans,
      La.   Card Index on Blacks in New Orleans, from newspapers
      covering the period 1850-1975.

707   Duke University Library, Durham, N. C. (Good manuscript col-
      lection on Blacks during Civil War and Post-Civil War
      Period).

708   Fisk University Library, Erastus Milo Cravath Memorial
      Library, Nashville, Tenn. Includes manuscripts collection.
      Restricted use: non-circulating. (Excellent collection on
      Black women).

709   Fort Valley State College, Henry Alexander Hunt Memorial
      Library, Fort Valley, Ga.

710   Free Library of Philadelphia, Social Science and History
      Department, Black Collection, Logan Square, Philadelphia,
      Penn.

711   Hampton Institute, Collis P. Huntington Memorial Library,
      George Foster Peabody Collection, Hampton, Va.

712   Howard University Moorland-Spingarn Research Center, Washington, D.C. (Excellent collection on Black women).

713   Jackson State University Library, Jackson, Mississippi. (Good collection on Black women).

714   Johnson Publishing Company Library, 1820 S. Michigan Ave., Chicago, Ill.

715   Lincoln University, Vail Memorial Library, Lincoln University, Penn. Includes African materials.

716   Livingstone College, Carnegie Library, Salisbury, N. C. The library has a Rare Book Room and out-of print books by and about Blacks, as well as other miscellaneous rare volumes and first editions. Restricted use: non-circulating. (Excellent collections on Black women).

717   New York Public Library Branch, Schomburg Research Library, 103 W. 135th Street, New York 10027. A library of books, periodicals, manuscripts, clippings, pictures, prints, records, and sheet music which attempts to record the entire experience of people of African descent--historical and contemporary. Restricted use: materials must be used on the premises.

718   North Carolina Central University Library, Black Collections, Durham, North Carolina.

719   Paine College, Warren A. Chandler Library, Augusta, Ga.

720   Philander Smith College Library, 812 West 13th St., Little Rock, Ark.

721   Richard B. Harrison Public Library, 214 S. Blount St., Raleigh, North Carolina. Mimeographed bibliographies available.

722   Rust College Library, Magee Memorial Library, Holly Springs, Miss.

723   Rutherford B. Hayes Library, 1337 Hayes Ave., Fremont, Ohio.

724   Savannah State College Library, Savannah, Ga. Includes pamphlet and clipping file.

725   Shaw University Library, Raleigh, North Carolina.

726   St. Augustine Seminary Library, Divine Word Seminary, Bay St. Louis, Miss. Maintained for missionary work among Blacks.

727   Stark Library, Benedict College, Taylor and Harden St.,
      Columbia, S. C. 29201.   Includes manuscripts, maps, pic-
      tures, slides.

728   Texas Southern University Library, Heartman Collection, 3201
      Wheeler, Houston, Tex.   Includes maps and photographs.

729   Tougaloo College, Wastman Library, Tougaloo, Miss.

730   Tuskegee Institute, Hollis Burke Frissell Library, Washington
      Collection, Tuskegee, Ala.

731   University of California (Santa Barbara), Wyles Collection,
      Goleta, California.   Emphasis primarily on the slave, and
      implications of slavery and the Civil War.

732   University of North Carolina, Louis Round Wilson Library,
      Chapel Hill, North Carolina.   (Good collection of manu-
      scripts on Blacks during Civil War and Post-Civil War
      Period).

733   Virginia Union University, William J. Clark Library, 1500
      Lombardy St., Richmond, Va.

734   Virginia State College Library, Norfolk Division, 2401
      Corprew Ave., Norfolk, Va.

735   Wilberforce University Library, James Weldon Johnson Memorial
      Collection of Black Arts and Letters, New Haven, Conn.
      Manuscripts and pictures.

736   Xavier University Library, Palmetto and Pine St., New Orleans,
      La.   Restricted use, closed August.   Manuscripts, maps, pic-
      tures, photostats, microfilm.   (Good collections on Black
      women).

NATIONAL ORGANIZATIONS OF BLACK WOMEN

737 ALPHA KAPPA ALPHA SORORITY, INC., 5211 South Greenwood Avenue, Chicago, Illinois 60615

738 BLACK NURSES ASSOCIATION, 792 Columbus Avenue, New York, New York 10025

739 BLACK SECRETARIES OF AMERICA, INC., P. O. Box 5581, Detroit, Michigan 48238

740 BLACK WOMEN'S COMMUNITY DEVELOPMENT FOUNDATION, 1028 Connecticut Avenue, N. W., Suite 1010, Washington, D. C. 20036

741 DELTA SIGMA THETA, INC., 1814 "M" Street, N. W., Washington, D. C. 20036

742 GAMMA PHI DELTA, 2927 Harper Street, Berkeley, California 94703

743 GIRL FRIENDS, INC., 449 East 79 Street, Chicago, Illinois 60619

744 IMPERIAL COURT, DAUGHTER OF ISIS, 3500 McDougall Avenue, Detroit, Michigan 48211

745 IOTA PHI LAMBDA SORORITY, INC., 1940 McClure Avenue, Youngstown, Ohio 44505

746 LADIES AUXILIARY OF NATIONAL DENTAL ASSOCIATIONS, INC., P. O. Box 197, Charlottesville, Virginia 22902

747 NATIONAL ASSOCIATION OF BARRISTERS' WIVES, c/o National Bar Association, Douglas State Bank Building, 1314 North 5th Street, Kansas City, Kansas 66101

748 NATIONAL ASSOCIATION OF COLORED WOMEN'S CLUBS, INC., 1601 R Street, N. W., Washington, D. C. 20009

749 NATIONAL ASSOCIATION OF MINISTER'S WIVES, INC., 7510 Beverley Road, Philadelphia, Pennsylvania 19138

750   NATIONAL ASSOCIATION OF NEGRO BUSINESS AND PROFESSIONAL
        WOMEN'S CLUBS, INC., 2861 Urban Avenue, Columbus, Ohio
        31907

751   NATIONAL BLACK SISTERS' CONFERENCE, 3333 5th Avenue, Pitts-
        burgh, Pennsylvania 15213

752   NATIONAL COUNCIL OF NEGRO WOMEN, INC., 1346 Connecticut
        Avenue, N. W., Suite 832, Washington, D.C. 20036

753   NATIONAL DOMESTIC WORKERS UNION OF AMERICA, 5 Forsyth Street,
        S. W., Atlanta, Georgia 30303

754   NATIONAL GRAND CHAPTER, ORDER OF EASTERN STAR, 1618 New
        Hampshire Avenue, Washington, D.C. 20009

755   NATIONAL HOUSEWIVES LEAGUE OF AMERICA, 539 Melbourne Street,
        Detroit, Michigan 48202

756   NATIONAL LINKS, INC. 118 Nelson Street, Durham, North
        Carolina 27707

757   SIGMA GAMMA RHO SORORITY, INC., 1254 25th Street, Indianap-
        olis, Indiana 46205

758   WOMEN'S AUXILIARY TO THE NATIONAL MEDICAL ASSOCIATION, 1627
        Mills "B" Lane Avenue, Savannah, Georgia 31405

759   ZETA PHI BETA SORORITY, INC., 1734 New Hampshire Avenue, N. W.
        Washington, D.C. 20009

NEWSPAPER PUBLISHERS AND EDITORS

Alabama

760   Beacon and Alabama Citizen
       Mrs. L. M. Thomas, Publisher, 2311 Coastarides, Mobile,
       Alabama 36601

761   Montgomery Mirror
       Mrs. Mildred Harris, Editor, 3061 Alta Road, Montgomery,
       Alabama 36110

Arizona

762   Arizona Tribune
       Mrs. Elouise H. Banks, Publisher and Editor, 2137 East
       Broadway Road, Phoenix, Arizona 85040

Arkansas

763   Southern Mediator Journal
       Mrs. C. H. Jones, Publisher, 213 Century Building, Little
       Rock, Arkansas 72203

California

764   Bakersfield Observer
       Nettie James, Editor, P. O. Box 2402, Bakersfield, Calif-
       ornia 93304

765   Firestone Park News and Southeast News Press
       Mrs. E. P. Alexander, Editor, Firestone, California 90007

766   Los Angeles Herald-Dispatch
       Mrs. E. P. Alexander, Editor, 1431 West Jefferson Boulevard,
       Los Angeles, California 90007

767   Los Angeles Watts Star Review
       Mrs. E. P. Alexander, Editor, 10817 1/2 Central Avenue,
       Los Angeles, California 90059

768   Stockton San Joaqium Progressor
       Miss Claudia Hudson, Editor, 235 South Stanislaus Street,
       Stockton, California 95201

769   Santa Anna Orange County Star Review
       Mrs. E. P. Alexander, Editor, 620 West Santa Anna
       Boulevard, Santa Anna, California 92701

Connecticut

770   Hartford Star
       Henry Morris, Editor, 701 Albany Avenue, Hartford,
       Connecticut 06112

Delaware

771   Wilmington Delaware Defender
       Miss A. G. Hibbert, Editor, 1400 French Street, Wilming-
       ton, Delaware 19801

District of Columbia

772   Washington Afro-American
       Mrs. Ruth Jenkins, Editor, 1800 11th Street, N. W.,
       Washington, D.C. 20001

Florida

773   Photo Illustrated News
       Mrs. M. A. Hall Williams, Publisher and Editor, 803 25th
       Street, West Palm Beach, Florida 33407

Georgia

774   Columbus Times
       Mrs. Ophelia Mitchele, Editor, 1304 Midway Drive,
       Columbus, Georgia 31906

Illinois

775   New Crusader
       Mrs. Dorothy R. Leavell, Publisher, 6429 South King Drive,
       Chicago, Illinois 60637

776 Woodlawn Observer
    Carolyn A. Fortier, Editor, 1133 East 63rd Street,
    Chicago, Illinois 60637

777 Maywood Suburban Echo-Reporter
    Mrs. Myrtle Jefferson, Editor, 1029 South 17th Avenue,
    Maywood, Illinois 60153

Indiana

778 New Crusader
    Mrs. Dorothy R. Leavell, Publisher, 1930 Broadway, Gary,
    Indiana 46407

Louisiana

779 Baton Rouge New Leader
    Mrs. Doris Gale, Editor, 196 South 14th Street, Baton
    Rouge, Louisiana 70802

780 Lake Charles News Leader
    Mrs. Rupert Clemmons, Editor, 112 Louisiana Street, Lake
    Charles, Louisiana 70601

781 Monroe News Leader
    Miss Geraldine Williams, Editor, 2301 DeSiard Street,
    Monroe, Louisiana 71203

Michigan

782 Kalamazoo Ledger
    Mrs. Jean Phillips, Publisher and Editor, P. O. Box 631,
    Kalamazoo, Michigan 49005

Minnesota

783 Twin Cities Courier
    Mary J. Kyle, Publisher, 84 South 6th Street, Minneapolis,
    Minnesota 55402

784 Twin Cities Observer
    Jeanne Cooper, Publisher and Editor, 23 South 6th Street,
    Minneapolis, Minnesota 55402

785 St. Paul Sun
    Jeanne Cooper, Publisher and Editor, 809 Dayton Avenue,
    St. Paul, Minnesota 55104

786   Minneapolis Twin Cities Courier
       Mary J. Kyle, Editor, 845 6th Street, Minneapolis,
       Minnesota 55402

Mississippi

787   Jackson Mississippi Enterprise
       Sarah Stevens, Editor, 110 East Monument, Jackson,
       Mississippi 39202

Missouri

788   The Call
       Mrs. Ada C. Franklin, Publisher, 1715 East 18th Street,
       Kansas City, Missouri 64108

789   Kansas City Call
       Miss Lucille Bluford, Editor, 1717 East 18th, Kansas City,
       Missouri 64108

Nebraska

790   Omaha Star
       Mrs. Mildred Brown, Publisher, 2216 North 24th Street,
       Omaha, Nebraska 68111

New York

791   Buffalo Challenger
       Mrs. Elaine Clark, Publisher and Editor, 1301 Fillmore,
       Buffalo, New York 14211

792   Jamaica New York Voice
       Miss Claire Paisner, Editor, 89-48 162nd Street, Jamaica,
       New York 11432

North Carolina

793   Carolina Times
       Vivian Austin Edmonds, Publisher, 436 East Pettigrew
       Street, Durham, North Carolina 27701

794   Lodius Austin, Editor, 436 East Pettigree Street, Durham,
       North Carolina 27701

Ohio

795   Cincinnati Herald
      Miss Marjorie Parham, Publisher, 836 Lincoln Avenue,
      Cincinnati, Ohio 45206

Oregon

796   Northwest Clarion Defender
      Mrs. Carl Bowele, Publisher, 319 N. E. Wygant, Portland,
      Oregon 97211

Pennsylvania

797   Afro-American Newspaper
      Mildred Neill, Editor, 4275 Broad Street, Philadelphia,
      Pennsylvania 19147

798   Philadelphia Nite Owl
      Mary Troupe, Publisher and Editor, 2728 West Girard
      Avenue, Philadelphia, Pennsylvania 19130

Texas

799   Fort Worth LaVida
      Audrey Pruit, Publisher and Editor, 3007 South Freeway,
      Fort Worth, Texas 76101

800   Houston Call
      Mrs. Ruby Palmer, Editor, 3430 Scott Street, Houston,
      Texas 77004

Wisconsin

801   Racine Star News
      Mrs. Carol Malone, Editor, 1436 State, Racine, Wisconsin
      53404

BLACK WOMEN ELECTED OFFICIALS

Alabama

802   Minnie Lee Brown
       Constable, Precinct 13
       Sumter County
       Boyd   35470

803   Britt Evans
       Constable, Beat 9
       Wilcox County
       Pine Apple 36768

804   Mrs. Mamie Foster
       Member, Board of Education
       2708 18th Place
       South Homewood   35209

805   Mrs. Connie H. Harper
       School Board Member
       Macon County
       Route 1, Box 197
       Shorter   36075

806   Mrs. S. T. Martin
       Tax Collector
       Macon County
       Tuskegee Institute 36088

807   Alma V. Miller
       Circuit Clerk
       Lowndes County
       P. O. Box 114
       Calhoun   36012

808   Eloise Montgomery
       Constable, Precinct 12
       Wilcox County
       General Delivery
       Snow Hill 36778

809   Alma R. Nelson
       Constable, Precinct 5
       Sumter County
       RFD
       York   36925

810   Mrs. Eletha Richardson
       Councilman
       Route 1, Box 476
       Ridgeville 35954

811   Cora L. Smith
       Docket Clerk
       Jefferson County
       4201 McClain Street
       Brighton   35020

812   Mrs. Willie Maud Snow
       Councilman
       Hobson City
       127 Park Avenue
       Anniston   36201

813   Marie Taylor
       Constable, Precinct 9
       Hale County
       Route 1, Box 54
       Newbern   36765

814   Bertha Thomas
       Constable, Beat 19
       Wilcos County
       Snow Hill 36778

815   Mrs. Katie Washington
       Councilman
       Geiger
       Route 1
       Emelle   35459

119

816   Mrs. Juanita Watson
Alderman
Brownville
2120 Avenue "K"
Bessemer 35020

817   Mrs. James R. Weatherly
Coroner
Sumter County
P. O. Drawer 580
York 36925

818   Mrs. Wadine Williams
Circuit Clerk
Greene County
Route 1, Box 164
Boligee 35443

819   Olivia Withcard
Constable, Precinct 7
Madison County
Route 3, Box 138-B
Madison 35758

820   Estella Witherspoon
Constable, Precinct 3
Wilcox County
Route 1, Box 72
Alberta 36720

Arizona

821   Ethel Williams
Member, Board of Trustees
Phoenix School District 1
Phoenix 85007

Arkansas

822   Mrs. Mabel Allen
School Board Member
Eudora Special School
  District
Chicot County
223 Arch Street
Eudora 71640

823   Mrs. Mary Carter
Justice of the Peace
Mississippi Township
Crittenden County
711 South 10th Street
West Memphis 72301

824   Mrs. A. S. Guinn
Town Clerk
Menifee 72107

825   Eula McGhee
Recorder
Reed 71670

826   Minnie Macklin
School Board Member
Sherrill School District
Jefferson County
General Delivery
Sherrill 72152

827   Mrs. Alice J. Martin
Recorder
1800 Cartwright Street
Norvell 72331

828   Margaret Martin
Justice of the Peace
Hill Township
Pulaski County
3600 Autumn Circle
Jacksonville 72076

829   Mrs. Lillian Morris
Justice of the Peace
Mississippi Township
Crittenden County
South 18th Street
West Memphis 72301

830   Mrs. Deborah Springer
Justice of the Peace
Pulaski County
2 Baltimore Street
Little Rock 72206

831   Vicie Lee Thompson
      School Board Member
      District 4
      Nevada County
      Route 2, Box 61
      Rosston   71858

832   Thelma Thrower
      School Board Member
      District 35
      Ouachita County
      247 Center Street
      Camden   71701

833   Phyllis Webb
      Alderman
      410 L. Street
      Wynne   72396

                  California

834   Mrs. Essie M. Brown
      School Board Member
      645 Grand Avenue
      Sacramento   95838

835   Mrs. Yvonne Barthwaite
         Burke
      United States
         Representative
      37th Congressional
         District, Los Angeles
      1027 Longworth House
         Office Building
      Washington, D.C.   20515

836   Mrs. Pearl Carey
      Councilman
      1231 Olympia
      Seaside   93995

837   Blanche N. Carter
      School Board Member
      2028 20th Street
      Apartment C
      Santa Monica   90404

838   Doris A. Davis
      City Clerk
      600 North Alameda
      Compton   90220

839   Bernice E. Fowler
      School Board Member
      89 Carolina Drive
      Benicia   94510

840   Mrs. Collie Gaines
      Councilman
      City Hall
      Marin City   94965

841   Mrs. Charlie Mae Haynes
      Member, Board of Education
      1832 16th Avenue
      San Francisco   94122

842   Mrs. Mary Jo Howell
      School Board Member
      1508 Albany Terrace
      Albany   94706

843   Mrs. Syrtiller Kabat
      School Board Member
      2209 Dumbarton Street
      East Palo Alto   94303

844   Thelma McKinney
      Marin City Community
         Services
      District Board Member
      30 Pacheco Street
      Marin City   94965

845   Mrs. Bettye R. Smith
      School Board Member,
         President
      1305 West Brazil Street
      Compton   90220

846   Mrs. Vivian Spearman
      School Board Member
      Fresno Colony
      Ivy Avenue
      Fresno   93706

847   Mrs. Vaino Spencer
      Judge, Superior Court
      110 North Grand Avenue
      Los Angeles   90012

848   Mrs. Betty Times
School Board Member
Sausalito School District
718 Drake Avenue
Marin City 94965

849   Ms. Doris Ward
Member, Board of Governors
San Francisco Community
   College
1333 Gough Street
San Francisco 94109

Colorado

850   Ada Evans
Mayor
City Hall
Fairplay

851   Mrs. Arie Taylor
Representative
District 17
831 East Las Animas
Colorado Spring 80903

Connecticut

852   Ernestine Brown
School Board Member
60 Home Avenue
Middletown 06457

853   Lillian O. Brown
Treasurer
244 Division Street
New Haven 06511

854   Mrs. Marcia Clinton
School Board Member
63 Pershing Street
Hartford 06112

855   Mrs. Virginia Cloud
Treasurer
City Hall
New Haven 06510

856   Mrs. Connie Collins
Alderman
242 Belden Street
New Britain 06051

857   Mrs. Shirley Gaskins
School Board Member
Board of Education
785 Park Avenue
Bloomfield 06002

858   Mrs. Fleeta Hudson
Member, Board of Education
1592 Stratford Avenue
Bridgeport 06607

859   Mrs. Jackie H. Lyles
Selectman and Justice of
   the Peace
220 Rockwell Avenue
Bloomfield 06002

860   Mrs. Rita Miller
Selectman
324 Jefferson Street
Bridgeport 06607

861   Lucille Moore
School Board Member
188 Cherry Street
Waterbury 06702

862   Mrs. Margaret E. Morton
Representative
District 94
25 Currier Street
Bridgeport 06607

863   Mrs. Mary H. Pittman
Zoning Board of Appeals
722 Blue Hills Avenue
Bloomfield 06002

864   Gail H. Stockham
School Board Member
190 Harding Avenue
Stratford 06497

865   Betty Swarz
Councilman
93 West Wooster Street
Danbury 06810

866   Mrs. Beatrice Wood
Councilman
131 Wadhams Road
Bloomfield 06002

Delaware

867 Mrs. Henrietta Johnson
Representative
District 3
1213 Lobdell Street
Wilmington   19801

868 Mrs. Hattie M. Phelan
Councilman
1035 Pine Street
Wilmington   19801

District of Columbia

869 Mrs. Hilda H. M. Mason
School Board Member
1459 Roxanna Road, N. W.
Washington, D.C.   20012

870 Virginia Morris
School Board Member
3107 W. Street, S. E.
Washington, D.C.   20020

871 Barbara Lett Simmons
School Board Member
7244 15th Place, N. W.
Washington, D.C.   20012

872 Mrs. Mattie G. Taylor
School Board Member
4016 19th Place, N. E.
Washington, D.C.   20018

Florida

873 Ms. Ester Berry
Commissioner
P. O. Box 585
South Bay   33493

874 Bobbie E. Brooks
Councilman, Council
   Chairman
1325 West 28th Street
Riviera Beach   33404

875 Ms. Gwendolyn Cherry
Representative
District 106
636 Northwest 2nd Avenue
Miami   33136

876 Mrs. Vernita Cox
Vice Mayor
P. O. Box 202
South Bay   33493

877 Bobbie Hunter
Councilman
P. O. Box 2163
Eatonville   32751

878 Mrs. May L. Singleton
Representative
District 16
1353 West 33rd Street
Jacksonville   32209

879 Ms. Earlene Watkins
Councilman
P. O. Box 2163
Eatonville   32751

Georgia

880 Mrs. Betty J. Clark
Representative
District 55
2293 Cresta Drive
Decatur   30032

881 Mrs. Delores Cook
School Board Member
Bibb County
3332 Pasadena Avenue
Macon   31201

882 Tollie Dobson
Justice of the Peace
Peace County
Perry Road
Fort Valley   31030

883   Mrs. Grace T. Hamilton
Representative
District 31
582 University Place,
  N. W.
Atlanta   30314

884   Bobbie L. Hill
Representative
District 110
Chatham County
458½ West Board Street
Savannah   31401

885   Edith J. Ingram
Judge, Court of Ordinary
Hancock County
718 New Street
Sparta   31087

886   Mrs. Carrie J. Mays
Councilman
1221 9th Street
Augusta   30901

Illinois

887   Mrs. JoAnn W. Brown
School Board Member
West Harvey District 147
15322 Lincoln
Harvey   60426

888   Mrs. Penny V. Brown
School Board Member
North Chicago Community
1426 Grove Avenue
North Chicago   60064

889   Mrs. Evelyn Burnett
School Board Member
1310 Ellis Drive
Urbana   61801

890   Cardiss Collins
United States
  Representative
7th Congressional
  District, Chicago
1610 Longworth Building
Washington, D.C.   20515

891   Thelma Demonbreun
School Board Member
14730 Lincoln Street
Harvey   60426

892   Mrs. Norma Eason
School Board Member
1802 Grey Avenue
Evanston   60201

893   Benita Griffis
Village Clerk
15147 Halsted Street
Harvey   60426

894   Kathryn B. Humphrey
School Board Member
716 Tawney Court
Champaign   61820

895   Eva Jones
School Board Member
1718 Wildwood
Bloomington   61701

896   Anna R. Langford
Alderman
City Hall
Chicago   60602

897   Mary McDade
School Board Member
3610 North Bredkenridge
  Court
Peoria   61614

898   Mrs. Peggy Smith Martin
Representative
District 26
6810 South Loomis
  Boulevard
Chicago   60636

899   Mrs. Edna Mason
Village Secretary
1327 Ellis Avenue
East Chicago Heights
  60411

900   Mrs. Edith Sampson
Judge, Circuit Court
1236 Madison Park
Chicago   60615

901   Esther V. Saverson
Alderman
232 North 61st Street
Centreville   62207

902   Mrs. Edna Summers
Alderman
1941 Heartrey Avenue
Evanston   60201

903   Dr. Florence Frye Winfield
School Board Member
Elementary District 65
1451 Fowler Avenue
Evanston   60201

904   Mrs. Ora Williams
School Board Member
Medger Evers School
10th & Lexington Avenue
East Chicago Heights
     60411

Indiana

905   Elizabeth Bridgewaters
School Board Member
925 West 7th Street
Bloomington   47401

906   Mrs. Julia Carson
Representative
District 45
2534 North Park Avenue
Indianapolis   46205

907   Mrs. Leculia Dent
Councilman-at-Large
2700 Jefferson Street
Gray   46402

908   Mrs. Henri Gibson
Councilman, District 9
City Hall
Indianapolis   46504

909   Mrs. Jessie Jacobs
School Board Member
419 West 40th Street
Indianapolis   46208

910   Mrs. Artricia Noel
Councilman, District 10
City Hall
Indianapolis   46504

Iowa

911   Mary Majors
Member, Board of Education
Lee County
424 North 12th Street
Keokuk   52632

Kansas

912   Mrs. Jo Brown
School Board Member
1550 North Madison
Wichita   67214

913   Mrs. James Ford
School Board Member
2330 Morgan Street
Parsons   67357

914   Sylvania Page
Councilman
712 Connecticut
Elwood   66024

915   Mrs. Bernice Terrell
School Board Member
406 North 10th Street
Elwood   66024

Kentucky

916   Dr. Joyce Howell
School Board Member
4th and Broadway Streets
Louisville   40202

917   Mrs. Mae Street Kidd
Representative
District 41
2308 West Chestnut
Louisville   40211

918 Rozelle Leavell
Councilman, Ward 1
914 East 1st Street
Hopkinsville 42240

919 Mrs. Charlotte S. McGill
Representative
District 42
3016 River Park Drive
Louisville 40211

920 Mrs. Lois Morris
Alderman
740 South 44th Street
Louisville 40211

921 Nora Motley
Councilman
420 Walnut Street
Lebanon 40033

922 Mrs. Georgia M. Davis
  Powers
Senator, District 33
733 Cecil Avenue
Louisville 40211

Louisiana

923 Hazel Batiste
School Board Member
Natchitoches Parish
P. O. Box 16
Natchitoches 71457

924 Dr. Ruth Bradford
Alderman
Box 28
Grambling 71245

925 Rosetta H. Days
Alderman
Box 482
Grambling 71245

926 Mrs. Helen B. Evans
School Board Member
Madison Parish
203 Stansbrough Street
Tallulah 71282

927 Mrs. Henrietta George
School Board Member
209 Magnolia Street
Monroe 71201

928 Agnes Hicks
Justice of the Peace
Franklin Parish
Winnsboro 71295

929 Mrs. Aza Lee Johnson
Justice of the Peace
Madison Parish
104 West Green Street
Tallulah 71282

930 Paulma Johnson
Member, Board of Education
St. Martin Parish School
 District
734 Jefferson Street
St. Martinville 70582

931 Mrs. Enice (Pat) Reed
School Board Member
District 2
St. Helena Parish
Route 2, Box 27
Greensburg 70441

932 Julia Mae Smith
Councilman
527 Haynes
Bastrop 71220

933 Corrine Colman Taylor
Member, Board of Education
Caddo Parish School
 District 15
4744 McDaniel Street
Shreveport 71101

934 Mrs. Dorothy Mae Taylor
Representative
District 93
2724 Melpomene
New Orleans 70113

935 Zelma C. Wyche
Chief of Police
500 East Green Street
Tallulah 71282

Maryland

936   Mrs. Mary B. Adams
Councilman
2414 Lafayette Avenue
Baltimore 21216

937   Mrs. Victorine Adams
Councilman
3103 Carlisle Avenue
Baltimore 21216

938   Ms. Hildegardeis Boswell
Delegate, District 4
1208 Druid Hill Avenue
Baltimore 21217

939   Rosetta Chase
Councilman
709 61st Avenue
Fairmont Heights 20027

940   Hattie Harrison
Delegate, District 2
2721 Mura Street
Baltimore 21213

941   Mrs. Evelyn McKenley
Councilman
54 Addison Road
Seat Pleasant 20027

942   Mrs. Lena K. Lee
Delegate, District 4
1818 Madison Avenue
Baltimore 21201

943   Elizabeth A. Trice
Councilman
8600 Glenarden Parkway
Glenarden 20801

944   Mrs. Verda F. Welcome
Senator, District 10
2101 Liberty Heights
   Avenue
Baltimore 21217

Massachusetts

945   Mrs. Doris Bunte
Representative
District 7
1106 Harrison Avenue
Boston 02119

946   Jane C. Edmonds
School Committeeman
36 Lantern Lane
Sharon 02067

947   Ms. Saundra Graham
Councilman
City Hall
Cambridge 02138

948   Leigh Potter
Member, Board of Health
Town Hall
Main Street
Mashpee 02649

949   Elizabeth Price
School Board Member
39 Sun Valley Drive
Worcester 06109

Michigan

950   Mrs. Bonita P. Branscumb
Commissioner
Buena Vista Street
Benton Harbor 49022

951   Mrs. Kathleen Bright
School Board Member
306 LaBelle Avenue
Highland Park 48203

952   Mrs. Marian E. Burch
Commissioner
Calhoun County
36 Greenwood Avenue
Battle Creek 49017

953   Ms. Hortense Canady
School Board Member
3808 West Holmes
Lansing   48912

954   Mrs. Josephine Carter
Clerk
Merrill Township
Bitely   49309

955   Ms. Vera Childress
Treasurer
Webber Township
Baldwin   49304

956   Gwen Clark
School Board Member
700 Seward
Detroit   48202

957   Ms. Barbara Rose Collins
School Board Member
Region #1 Office
North Carolina Mutual
   Building
8401 Woodward Avenue
Detroit   48202

958   Mrs. Phillis Cook
School Board Member
Board of Education
27385 West Outer Drive
Ecrose   48229

959   Ms. Daisy Elliot
Representative
District 8
8701 LaSalle Boulevard
Detroit   48206

960   Ms. Rosetta Ferguson
Representative
District 20
2676 Arndt
Detroit   48207

961   Geraldine Bledsoe Ford
Judge, Recorder's Court
1441 St. Antoine Street
Detroit   48226

962   Mary E. Gilmore
School Board Member
4852 Cope
Detroit   48215

963   Mrs. Alvene Grice
School Board Member
Covert   49043

964   Mrs. Helen Harris
School Board Member
1632 Kensington Street
Flint   48503

965   Ms. Erma Henderson
Councilman
City-County Building
2 Woodward Avenue
Detroit   48226

966   Ms. Patricia Hoskins
Clerk
Yates Township
Idlewild   49642

967   Lula Lee
Commissioner
Berrian County
415 Miller Street
Benton Harbor   49022

968   Ms. Blanche Martin
Member, Board of Trustees
Michigan State University
1999 Winchester
East Lansing   48823

969   Dr. Elizabeth Minott
Commissioner
Berrian County
980 Bishop
Benton Harbor   49022

970   Blanche Moon
Trustee
Idlewild   49642

971   Mrs. Elnora Moorman
Commissioner
Jackson County
1120 South Milwaukee
Jackson   49203

972   Mrs. Ida Murray
      School Board Member
      6081 Vancourt
      Detroit   48120

973   Mrs. Mary Neal
      Supervisor
      Yates Township
      Box 23
      Idlewild   49642

974   Ms. Clara W. Rutherford
      Member, Central Board of
        Education
      City of Detroit
      2710 Tuxedo Avenue
      Detroit   48206

975   Ms. Catherine Shavers
      Commissioner
      Wayne County
      902 City-County Building
      2 Woodward Avenue
      Detroit   48226

976   Dr. Mildred B. Smith
      Member, Board of Regents
      Eastern Michigan
        University
      Ypsilanti   48197

977   Mrs. Alma G. Stallworth
      Representative
      District 4
      18301 Birchwood
      Detroit   48221

978   Mrs. Ethel Terrell
      Councilman
      30 Gerald Avenue
      Highland Park   48203

979   Mrs. Charlotte Paige
        Tucker
      Treasurer
      Merrill Township
      Bitely   49309

980   Charlotte L. Williams
      Commissioner
      Gemessee County
      2030 Barks Street
      Flint   48503

Mississippi

981   Julia A. Banks
      Election Commissioner
      District 4
      Jefferson County
      Route 1, Box 117
      Fayette   39069

982   Rosemore Boyd
      School Board Member
      District 5
      Madison County
      Route 2
      Camden   39045

983   Marjorie Brandon
      Justice of the Peace,
        Beat 1
      Claiborne County
      Route 1, Box 149
      Port Gibson   39150

984   Lillie Brown
      School Board Member
      Jefferson County
      General Delivery
      Fayette   39069

985   Julia Matilda Burns
      School Board Member
      Holmes County
      Route 2, Box 141
      Tchula   39169

986   Annyce Campbell
      Alderman
      P. O. Box 333
      Mound Bayou   38762

987   Mildred Coleman
      Justice of the Peace
      Jefferson County
      General Delivery
      Lorman   39096

988   Ester Dixon
      City Election Commissioner
      P. O. Box 7
      Bolton   39041

989 Marie Green
School Board Member
Wilkinson County
Route 2, Box 938
Woodville 39669

990 Helen R. Harris
Town Clerk
Tax Assessor Collector
P. O. Box 7
Bolton 39041

991 Estella Heard
City Election Commissioner
P. O. Box 7
Bolton 39041

992 Mary Slate Huddleston
Alderman
P. O. Box 145
Mound Bayou 38762

993 Etta Hudson
City Election Commissioner
General Delivery
Fayette 39069

994 Hattie Hullitt
City Election Commissioner
P. O. Box 7
Bolton 39041

995 Dorothy A. Humphrey
Alderman
General Delivery
Fayette 39069

996 Clara Jackson
City Election Commissioner
General Delivery
Fayette 39069

997 Maggie Jackson
City Election Commissioner
General Delivery
Fayette 39069

998 Mrs. Elra Johnson
Election Commissioner
Holmes County
100 Hines Street
Durant 39063

999 Sarah Johnson
Councilman
1952 Michigan Street
Greenville 38701

1000 Eartha M. Jones
City Election Commissioner
P. O. Box 7
Bolton 39041

1001 Julia Jones
Clerk, Circuit of Court
Claiborne County
P. O. Box 549
Port Gibson 39150

1002 Ellen King
City Election Commissioner
General Delivery
Fayette 39069

1003 Lillie Lee
City Election Commissioner
District 3
General Delivery
Fayette 39069

1004 Ms. Matiel Lewis
City Election Commissioner
General Delivery
Fayette 39069

1005 Dr. Arenia C. Mallory
School Board Member
Holmes County
Box 419
Lexington 39095

1006 Essie Morrow
School Board Member
East Jasper Consolidated
  School District
General Delivery
Heidelburg 39439

1007 Flotilla S. Norman
Alderman
P. O. Box 13
Winstonville 38781

1008   Dianne Robinson
City Election Commissioner
P. O. Box 7
Bolton 39041

1009   Marie Rollins
City Election Commissioner
P. O. Box 7
Bolton 39041

1010   Mary H. Russ
Justice of the Peace
District 1
Wilkinson County
Route 2, Box 487
Centreville 39631

1011   Bertha W. Sanders
Clerk
General Delivery
Winstonville 38781

1012   Lillie M. Shaw
Alderman
P. O. Box 55
Falcon 38628

1013   Ms. Eddie Lou Smith
Justice of the Peace
Madison County
Route 4, Box 305
Canton 39046

10__   Lena Witherspoon
Alderman
P. O. Box 50
Winstonville 38781

Missouri

1015   Mrs. Garnette M. Adams
School Board Member
Wellston Board of
   Education
6467 Plymouth
St. Louis 63133

1016   Louvenia H. Boyd
School Board Member
Wellston Board of
   Education
6467 Plymouth
St. Louis 63133

1017   Mrs. DeVerne L. Calloway
Representative
District 81
4309 Enright Avenue
St. Louis 63108

1018   Bessie Cole
City Collector
Howardville 63869

1019   Louise W. Cooper
City Collector
Hayti Collector
P. O. Box 426
Hayti 63851

1020   Delores Glover
Alderman
4535 Fair Avenue
St. Louis 63115

1021   Delores Haynes
President, School Board
Wellston Board of
   Education
6159 Suburban Avenue
St. Louis 63133

1022   Geneva Hayes
Alderman
5805 Selber Street
St. Louis 63120

1023   Ernestine Hinton
Alderman
City Hall
1206 Market Street
St. Louis 63103

1024   Laura Howard
City Treasurer
Howardville 63869

1025   Mamie F. Hughes
County Legislator
Jackson County
1763 Woodland Avenue
Kansas City   64109

1026   Daisy McFowland
Alderman
4150 Massitt
St. Louis   63113

1027   Adella T. Smiley
School Board Member
7 Windermere Place
St. Louis   63112

1028   Mrs. L. T. Tallie
Tax Collector
City Hall
Kinloch   63140

1029   Joann Wayne
Alderman
5815 Highland Avenue
St. Louis   63112

Nevada

1030   Bernice Moten
Trustee
Clark County School Board
401 Recco
North Las Vegas   80930

New Jersey

1031   Mrs. Almerth Battle
Councilman
507 Mayfair Lane
Neptune   07753

1032   Mattie Bowser
School Board Member
West Berlin Township
Myrtle Avenue
Berlin   08009

1033   Pauline Boykin
School Board Member
Fairfield Township
85 South Avenue
Bridgeton   08302

1034   Alice B. Carter
School Board Member
15 North Connecticut
Avenue
Atlantic City   08401

1035   Elizabeth Chitty
Member, Board of Education
1228 South End Parkway
Plainfield   07060

1036   Kathleen M. Edwards
School Board Member
526 Stockton Street
Princeton   08540

1037   Rosetta Finkenhoffe
School Board Member
Borough Hall
Chesilhurst   08049

1038   Thelma K. Gaddis
Vice President, School
Board
P. O. Box 674
Asbury Park   07712

1039   Margaret Garvin
School Board Member
188 Fulton Street
New Brunswick   08902

1040   Beatrice Jenkins
Councilman-at-Large
Welmore Avenue
Morristown   07960

1041   Janet Johnson
School Board Member
521 4th Street
Palmyra   08065

1042   Katherine M. Kitchart
        Vice President, School
          Board
        90 East Burlington Street
        Bordentown 08505

1043   Wynona M. Lipman
        Senator, District 29
        50 Park Place
        Newark 07102

1044   Vivian B. Makle
        School Board Member
        32 Park End Place
        East Orange 07018

1045   Ms. Acquilla Matthews
        President, Board of
          Education
        133 North Pennsylvania
          Avenue
        Atlantic City 08401

1046   Annie R. Mersereau
        School Board Member
        118 Congress Avenue
        Teaneck 07666

1047   Lula Moss
        School Board Member
        Oaks Avenue
        Lawnside 08045

1048   Mary A. Nelson
        Tax Collector
        160 East Oak Avenue
        Lawnside 08045

1049   Marguerite Page
        School Board Member
        220 Passaic Street
        Passaic 07055

1050   Margaret Parker
        School Board Member
        76 Branch Avenue
        Red Bank 07701

1051   Mrs. Morice Portee
        Councilman
        Garfield Avenue
        Chesilhurst 08049

1052   Iva Smith
        School Board Member
        Third & Washington Avenues
        Chesilhurst 08049

1053   Dr. Jeanne A. Smith
        School Board Member
        347 Webster Avenue
        Englewood 07631

1054   Nellie F. Suratt
        Councilman, Ward 4
        306 Halsey Street
        Plainfield 07063

1055   Nancy Thomas
        School Board Member
        145 Reade Street
        Englewood 07631

1056   Bertha Upshaw
        School Board Member
        Thomas Avenue
        Lawnside 08045

1057   Marilyn S. Vaughn
        School Board Member
        1230 Brookside Road
        Piscataway 08854

New York

1058   Bessie M. Berry
        School Board Member
        123 Piermont Avenue
        Elmira 14905

1059   Marie Bethea
        School Board Member
        Luty Drive
        Hyde Park 12538

1060   Elizabeth Bond
        Member, Community School
          Board
        District 16
        94 Ralph Avenue
        Brooklyn 11221

1061   Shirle Brown
School Board Member
District 4
346 East 117th Street
New York   10033

1062   Lillian Carter
Member, Community School
   Board
District 23
320 Rockaway Avenue
Brooklyn   11233

1063   Shirley A. Chisholm
United States
   Representative
12th Congressional
   District, Brooklyn
123 Cannon House Office
   Building
Washington, D.C.   20515

1064   Mary Cooper
Member, Community School
   Board
District 13
44 Court Street
Brooklyn   11201

1065   Mary Ellen Cooper
School Board Member
353 Fourth Avenue
Mount Vernon   10550

1066   Estella B. Diggs
Assemblyman, District 78
592 East 167th Street
Bronx   10456

1067   Iona Edwards
School Board Member
District 6
501 Courtlandt Avenue
New York   10451

1068   Betty Louise Felton
School Board Member
District 25
70-30 164th Street
Flushing   11365

1069   Marquette Floyd
Judge, District Court
Suffolk County
Babylon   11702

1070   Lucille Greene
Member, Community School
   Board
District 23
320 Rockaway Avenue
Brooklyn   11233

1071   Edith Hicks
School Board Member
District 9
1377 Jerome Avenue
New York   10452

1072   Jeanette Hughes
Member, Community School
   Board
District 16
1010 Lafayette Avenue
Brooklyn   11221

1073   Katherine J. James
School Board Member
District 28
114-32 158th Street
Jamaica   11434

1074   Eloise Krause
School Board Member
District 12
708 East Tremont Avenue
New York   10457

1075   Shirley Lee
Member, Community School
   Board
District 19
590 New Lots Avenue
Brooklyn   11207

1076   Marjorie Matthews
Member, Bedford Stuyvesant
   Community School Board
District 16
1010 Lafayette Avenue
Brooklyn   11221

1077   Eunica Mattis
        School Board Member
        District 9
        1377 Jerome Avenue
        New York   10452

1078   Grace E. Morton
        Secretary, School Board
        District 3
        164 West 97th Street
        New York   10025

1079   Mary Norris
        School Board Member
        District 4
        346 East 117th Street
        New York   10033

1080   Delia Ortiz
        President, Community School
           Board
        District 5
        433 West 123rd Street
        New York   10027

1081   Claire Thomas Pearce
        President, Community School
           Board
        District 13
        Brooklyn   11201

1082   Mary Pinkett
        Councilman, Borough of
           Brooklyn
        309 Lafayette Avenue
        New York   11238

1083   Dr. Gerta Rainsford
        School Board Member
        312 Greenwich Street
        Hempstead   11550

1084   Alama Sanders Roman
        Vice President, East
           Ramapo Central School
           District
        Camp Hill Road
        Pomona   10971

1085   Mary A. Saunders
        Vice President, Community
           School Board
        District 6
        665 West 182nd Street
        New York   10033

1086   Pearline Skeeter
        Secretary, Community School
           Board
        District 5
        443 West 123rd Street
        New York   10027

1087   Edith Smith
        School Board Member
        District 12
        708 East Tremont Avenue
        New York   10457

1088   Constance Timberlake
        Commissioner, Board of
           Education
        Solcum Hall
        Syracuse University
        Syracuse   13210

1089   Laura Valdes
        School Board Member
        District 11
        Parchester House
        11 Metropolitan Oval
        Bronx   10462

1090   Elizabeth Williams
        Member, Community School
           Board
        District 5
        433 West 123rd Street
        New York   10027

North Carolina

1091   Elreta Melton Alexander
        Judge, State District
           Court, District 18
        Guilford County
        Guilford County Courthouse
        Greensboro   27402

1092 Miss Zoe Barebee
Guilford County
  Commissioner
Guilford County
Guilford County Courthouse
Greensboro 27402

1093 Mary Elizabeth Black
Commissioner
Princeville
P. O. Box 485
Tarboro 27886

1094 Elizabeth B. Cofield
Commissioner
Wake County
2322 Wade Avenue
Raleigh 27601

1095 Helen Cooper
Member, Board of Education
Bertie County
Route 1, Box 306
Windsor 27983

1096 Mary T. Eldridge
Member, Board of Education
Cumberland County
1877 Brodell Drive
Fayetteville 28301

1097 Ethel T. Hayswood
Member, Board of Education
Robeson County
Willow Street
Lumberton 28358

1098 Leslie W. Holley
Member, Board of Education
Edgecombe County
Route 1, Box 108
Battleboro 27809

1099 Nettie G. Metton
Councilman
P. O. Box 24
Cofield 27922

1100 Mamie Pittman
Commissioner
Princeville
701 Green Boulevard
Tarboro 27886

1101 Leslie Dewey Strayhorn
Member, Board of Education
Jones County
P. O. Box 61
Trenton 28585

1102 Mary Elizabeth Tolsome
Member, Board of Education
Route 2
St. Pauls 28384

Ohio

1103 Lillian W. Burke
Judge, Municipal Court
Lakeside & Ontario
Cleveland 44114

1104 Carrie Cain
Councilman
City Hall
601 Lakeside Avenue
Cleveland 44114

1105 Betty Chapman
School Board Member
505 Knickerbocker Avenue
Springfield 45506

1106 Grace Cooley
Trustee, Board of Public
  Affairs
3765 Third Avenue
Urbancrest 43123

1107 Ellen Walker Craig
Mayor
2879 Walnut Street
Urbancrest 43123

1108 Vivian J. Larkins
Councilman
3584 Central Avenue
Urbancrest 43123

1109 Carol A. McLendon
Councilman
City Hall
601 Lakeside Avenue
Cleveland 44114

1110   Mildred Madison
        Councilman
        City Hall
        891 East Boulevard
        Cleveland 44108

1111   Mildred Madison
        Member, State Board of
            Education
        891 East Boulevard
        Cleveland 44108

1112   Sophia Mitchell
        Mayor
        Box 114
        Rendsville 43775

1113   Betty J. Perry
        Councilman
        Village Hall
        27899 Chagrin Boulevard
        Woodmere 44122

1114   Myrtle K. Rush
        Councilman
        222 Grove Road
        Woodlawn 45215

1115   Mae Steward
        City Commissioner
        1252 Melbourne Road
        East Cleveland 44112

1116   Mrs. Onetha Trammer
        Clerk-Treasurer
        Village Hall
        27899 Chagrin Boulevard
        Woodmere 44122

1117   Dolores Ziglar
        Councilman
        2818 Main Street
        Urbancrest 43123

Oklahoma

1118   Jane Anderson
        Secretary, Board of
            Trustees
        City Hall
        Langston 73050

1119   Hannah D. Atkins
        Representative
        District 97
        Route 4, Box 799
        Oklahoma City 73111

1120   Maud C. Brown
        Treasurer, Board of
            Trustees
        City Hall
        Langston 73050

1121   Thelma Chandler
        School Board Member
        2301 Dennison Street
        Muskogee 74401

1122   Carrie Culton
        School Board Member
        Taft
        Route 1, Box 417
        Muskogee 74401

1123   Selma Drakes
        Councilman
        Clearview 74835

1124   Josephine Gaines
        Treasurer
        General Delivery
        Tullahassee 74459

1125   Leona Hall
        Town Clerk
        Box 606
        Boley 74829

1126   Jean Haynes
        Trustee
        City Hall
        Langston 73050

1127   Viola Howell
        Alderman
        General Delivery
        Tullahassee 74466

1128   Fanny B. Martin
        School Board Member
        Box 296
        Taft 74463

1129 Susie Nears
Councilman
P. O. Box 55
Rentiesville 74459

1130 Ms. Avalm B. Reece
Councilman
927 South Main
Muskogee 74401

1131 Gloiretta Russell
Clerk
Town Hall
Taft 74463

1132 Gladys Teagues
School Board Member
Taft 74463

1133 Emma L. Walton
Town Clerk
Tullahassee 74459

1134 Ernestine Young
Clerk
Town Hall
Brooksville 74801

1135 Louise M. Young
School Board Member, Clerk
P. O. Box 234
Boley 74829

Oregon

1136 Mrs. Mercedes F. Deiz
Judge, Circuit Court
320 County Court House
Portland 97204

1137 Gladys McCoy
School Board Member
6650 North Amherst Street
Portland 97230

Pennsylvania

1138 Dr. Ethel Allen
Councilman, District 8
2303 West Nicholas Street
Philadelphia 19121

1139 Pauline R. Davis
School Board Member
727 Cedar Street
Bristol 19007

1140 Doris M. Harris
Judge, Court of Common
Pleas
District 1
1503 One East Penn Square
Building
Philadelphia 19107

1141 Mrs. Nevada Murray
Jury Commissioner
R. D. 1, Beacon Hill Road
Doylestown 18901

1142 Isabelle Ramseur
Councilman
228 North 10th Street
Darby 19023

1143 Geneva Roane
School Board Member
2121 West 4th Street
Chester 19017

1144 Juanita Kidd Stout
Judge, Court of Common
Pleas
District 1
City Hall
Philadelphia 19107

1145 Bernice Lee Vaughn
School Board Member
1805 Cornell Street
McKeesport 15130

Rhode Island

1146   Rosalyn McDonald
Chairman, School Board
275 Cindy Ann Drive
East Greenwich 02818

South Carolina

1147   Mrs. Eddie Ruth Brawley
Councilman
P. O. Box 145
Eastover 29044

1148   Olivia Cohen
Councilman
General Delivery
Fairfax 29827

1149   Thelma Cook
Magistrate
Fairfield County
Route 3, Box 190
Winnsboro 29180

1150   Mary Glas
Councilman
c/o City Hall
Atlantic Beach 29531

1151   Dorothy Hart
Councilman
c/o City Hall
Atlantic Beach 29531

1152   Frieda R. Mitchell
School Board Member
Beaufort County
P. O. Box 19
Sheldon 29941

1153   Agnes C. Sherman
School Board Member
Beaufort County
P. O. Box 93
Frogmore 29920

1154   Hattie Sims
Magistrate
Richland County
Route 1, Box 166-B
Hopkins 29061

Tennessee

1155   Emily C. Brown
Justice of the Peace
Williamson County
957 Glass Street
Franklin 37064

1156   Lois DeBerry
Representative
District 91
1373 Valse Street
Memphis 38106

1157   Mrs. Lorenzo Collier
Magistrate
Mongomery County
1150 College Street
Clarksville 37047

1158   Sarah Moore Greene
School Board Member
2453 Linden Avenue, S. E.
Knoxville 37917

1159   Bettye Jean Jones
Member, Democratic Executive Committee
District 3
Shelby County
Memphis 38126

1160   Lettie M. Parker Kendall
Magistrate
Montgomery County,
District 13
388 A. Street
Clarksville 37040

1161   Ms. James Deotha Malone
Vice Mayor
229 South Pardue Avenue
Gallatin 37066

1162   Jean Palmer
Magistrate
Henry County
403 Rison Street
Paris 38242

1163 Leola Parks
School Board Member
Knox County
2141 Riverside Drive
Knoxville 37915

1164 Isabelle K. Roberts
Magistrate
Rutherford County
Murfreesboro 37130

1165 Shelvie Rose
Magistrate
Tipton County
Court House
Covington 38019

1166 Maxine Smith School
School Board Member
1208 East Parkway, South
Memphis 38114

Texas

1167 Wilhelmina Delco
School Board Member
Austin ISD
Travis County
1805 Astor Place
Austin 78721

1168 Mrs. Clarence L. Ervin
School Board Member
Lubbock ISD
Lubbock County
2806 Walnut Avenue
Lubbock 79404

1169 Barbara Lee Ewing
Councilman
958-3 San Antonia Avenue
Sequin 78155

1170 Mrs. Eddie Bernice Johnson
Representative
District 33-0
2107 Lanark Avenue
Dallas 75203

1171 Arlene Jordan
School Board Member
Cleveland ISD
Liberty County
1240 Rusk Street
Cleveland 77327

1172 Barbara C. Jordan
United States
Representative
18 Congressional District,
Houston
1725 Longworth House
Office Building
Washington, D.C. 20515

1173 Lucy P. Patterson
Councilman
2779 Almeda Drive
Dallas 75216

1174 Artie Mae White
School Board Member
North Forest ISD
Harris County
7968 Cinderella Street
Houston 77028

Virginia

1175 Iona W. Adkins
County Clerk
Charles City County
Charles City 23030

1176 Ruth Harvey Charity
Councilman
453 South Main Street
Danville 24551

1177 Ms. Willie Jones Dell
Councilman
c/o City Clerk
1001 East Broad Street
Richmond 23219

1178 Mattie Lee Gholson
Justice of the Peace
Dinwiddie County
Church Road 23833

1179   Alma Gibbs
Councilman
P. O. Box 227
Dendron   23939

1180   Elizabeth E. Johnson
Justice of the Peace
Madison District
Cumberland County
RFD 2, Box 7
Cumberland   23040

1181   Mrs. Jessie M. Rattley
Councilman
529 Ivy Avenue
Newport News   23607

Washington

1182   Peggie Joan Maxie
Representative
District 37
Seattle   98122

West Virginia

1183   Earline Tate
Councilman
Main Street
Osage   26543

Wyoming

1184   Alberta Johnson
Councilman
P. O. Box 961
Cheyenne   82001

1185. BLACK WOMEN IN RURAL AREAS: STATISTICS*

	Total
Rural United States	2,121,888

Regions
    Northeast   57,836
    North Central   53,830
    South   1,990,688
    West   19,532

Northeast
    New England   6,635
    Middle Atlantic   15,201

North Central
    East North Central   38,642
    West North Central   15,188

South
    South Atlantic   1,090,978
    East South Central   510,834
    West South Central   388,876

West
    Mountain   3,867
    Pacific   15,665

*Source: Bureau of the Census (1970)

1186. BLACK WOMEN IN URBAN AREAS: STATISTICS*

	Total
Urban United States	9,710,087

Regions

Northeast	2,259,373
North Central	2,335,499
South	4,277,171
West	838,044

Northeast

New England	197,237
Middle Atlantic	2,062,136

North Central

East North Central	1,986,690
West North Central	348,809

South

South Atlantic	2,244,906
East South Central	847,417
West South Central	1,184,848

West

Mountain	83,810
Pacific	754,234

*Source: Bureau of the Census (1970)

INDEX

Including subjects, authors, joint authors, compilers and
editors. Numbers refer to the individual entry number.

Abdul, Raoul, 1
Abolitionist Movement, 64, 69,
  106
Abolitionist, 64, 69, 106, 225,
  228, 234, 293, 363, 481
Abortion, 312
Accompong, Jamaica, 96
Actresses, 1, 17, 173, 242, 290,
  291, 444, 545
Adams, Effie Kay, 2
Adams, Elizabeth Laura, 3
Adams, Garnette M., 1015
Adams, John H., Jr., 306
Adams, Mary B., 936
Adams, Victorine, 937
Adkins, Iona W., 1175
Adoff, Arnold, 4
Adoption, 407, 608, 609, 612,
  616, 623
Africa, 10, 12, 14, 39, 41, 249,
  253, 268
Albert, Octavia Victoria Rogers,
  5
Albertson, Chris, 6
Alderman, See E.O.
Aldous, Joan, 307
Alexander, Elreta Melton, 1091
Alexander, E. P., 765, 766, 767,
  769
Alexander, William T., 7
Allen, Dr. Ethel, 1138
Allen, Mabel, 822
Alpha Kappa Alpha Sorority, 8,
  220, 334, 737
Anderson, Jane, 1118

Anderson, Marion, 9
Anderson, Rosa Claudett, 10
Andrews, Roberta G., 309
Angelou, Maya, 11, 12
Anthologies, 75, 79, 569, 576,
  590
Anthony, Mary, 310
Aptheker, Bettina, 13, 84
Aptheker, Herbert, 311
Armistead, Wilson, 14
Army, 157, 209, 386, 560
Artists, 15, 16, 108, 117, 120,
  167, 181, 231, 242, 279, 345,
  461, 559
Ashe, Christy, 312
Assemblyman, See E.O.
Atkins, Hannah D., 1119
Atkinson, J. Edward, 15
Atlanta University, 5
Austin, Lodius, 794
Autobiography, 1-305
Avery, Paul, 313
Atlanta, Georgia, 5

Bailey, Leaonead Pack, 16
Bailey, Pearl, 17, 18, 19, 314
Baker, Joseph V., 315
Banks, Elouise H., 762
Banks, Julia A., 981
Baraka, Imaum Amiri, 316
Barebe, Zoe, 1092
Barlow, Leila Mae, 20
Baskin, Wade, 21
Bass, Charlotta A., 22
Bates, Daisy, 23

INDEX

INDEX

INDEX